M000288601

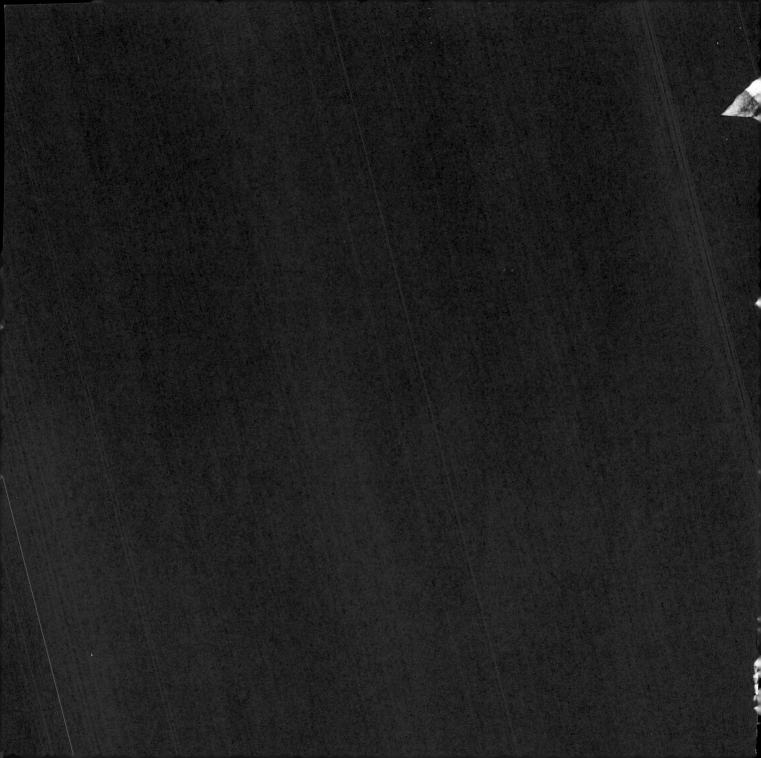

GOLD
WINE

To the farmers
and producers
who champion hyperlocal,
indigenous ingredients.
You are the keepers
of the flame of our
culinary heritage.
Keep on rockin'…

NOAH CHARNEY

GOLD
WINE

Rebula, the Liquid Gold
That Links Slovenia and Italy

ROWMAN & LITTLEFIELD
Lanham • Boulder • New York • London

Author: NOAH CHARNEY

Photos: DAMIJAN SIMČIČ, MANUEL KOVŠCA,
MARIJAN MOČIVNIK, MATIC GRMEK, DEAN DUBOKOVIČ,
ALEŠ BENO, NEBOJŠA BABIČ, SUZAN GABRIJAN, MATJAŽ TANČIČ,
MANCA JEVŠČEK, VESNA KRISTANČIČ, LOREDANA BENSA

Map: URŠKA CHARNEY

Design: ŽARE KERIN / FUTURA DDB

Typesetting: MARJAN BOŽIČ / FUTURA DDB

Proofreading: JOSH ROCCHIO

Translations: URŠKA CHARNEY

1st edition

Published by Rowman & Littlefield

An imprint of The Rowman & Littlefield Publishing Group, Inc.

4501 Forbes Boulevard, Suite 200, Lanham, Maryland 20706

www.rowman.com

86-90 Paul Street, London EC2A 4NE

Copyright © 2023 by The Rowman & Littlefield Publishing Group, Inc.

All rights reserved. No part of this book may be reproduced in any form or by any electronic or mechanical means, including information storage and retrieval systems, without written permission from the publisher, except by a reviewer who may quote passages in a review.

British Library Cataloguing in Publication Information Available

Library of Congress Cataloging-in-Publication Data Available

ISBN: 978-1-5381-6651-2 (hardcover)

ISBN: 978-1-5381-6652-9 (electronic)

♾™ The paper used in this publication meets the minimum requirements of American National Standard for Information Sciences—Permanence of Paper for Printed Library Materials, ANSI/NISO Z39.48-1992.

Printed in Mumbai, India

TABLE OF CONTENTS

FOREWORD

I have long been fascinated by the way wine provides a great lens to view and connect with a place. In just one glass, it can tell the story of the landscape, aspect, soils, climate and weather, but more than that, it also reflects the history and culture of the hands that created it. This book is the tale of how all that is brought together through the medium of one grape: Rebula, and how one man - Zvonimir "Miro" Simčič - shaped its history and place in the world today.

Brda/Collio is a stunningly beautiful cross-border region, historically a single region divided after WWII. Both the Slovenian and Italian names mean "hilly," and the landscape lives up to this name, full of green hillsides covered in vines with a backdrop of snow-tipped Julian Alps. 85% of Brda's vineyards are on steep slopes and terraces, and in between the vines, the vineyards buzz with wildlife - sustainability is an important philosophy here.

I firmly believe in Rebula (aka Ribolla Gialla) as a grape, seeing its quality in the glass through many tastings with winemakers from Brda and Collio over the years. I'm also panel chair for this region at the prestigious Decanter World Wine Awards which gives an independent view of the quality of the wines. At the 2020 competition, for instance, Rebula picked up 14 gold, silver or platinum medals.

So why do local grapes matter when there is plenty of great Chardonnay or Sauvignon out there? What a local grape offers is a point of difference in a world seeking new experiences. A good local grape is authentic, well suited to local growing conditions and may have a long history in the area and can deliver a sense of place which helps connect wine purchasers to a region. But there's no doubt this is also a challenge - promoting a grape no one has heard of, from a place no one knows. It requires support from the domestic market too, where younger generations may prefer the glamor of international grapes over what their parents and grandparents drank.

Rebula can offer all this: delivering good-to-great quality wines with that all-important sense of place. The grape also has a track record back to the 14th century which gives credibility and shows that Rebula is not just a flash-in-the-pan. The earliest credible references to the Rebula/Ribolla grape appear in ecclesiastical records from the 13th century and there are many reports that it was highly regarded and was a favorite of the aristocracy, as well as being used as payment in kind to settle debts.

I also see Rebula as a grape with a bit of a rebellious streak. It's hung on, with Miro's help, in Slovenia's western region of Brda in the face of natural and economic crises such as phylloxera, two world wars and the aftermath – Yugoslavian politics. In Slovenia, it stood firm in the face of the global march of international varieties and today is planted on 371 ha in Brda (21% of the region). It also has a stubborn nature in its ability to deliver its best fruit when fighting for life on steep slopes and dry, rocky soils, especially with its favored *opoka* soils (*ponca* in Italy).

Amongst all the 1500 or more grapes grown in the world for wine, some have fallen out of favor for good reasons: difficult to cultivate, poor quality, disease-prone and so on. However, in other cases cultural changes and politics have been more to blame. It's always required a person (like Miro) to rescue such grapes from obscurity; to champion and cultivate and work out whether there really is quality potential. For me, there's only a short list of these hyper-local varieties that have been worth re-rehabilitating, and Rebula is one.

One of the things I love about the grape is its incredible versatility - offering quality and, importantly, enjoyment across all its styles. Each of these has a place in the world of wine drinking. The fresh, fruity, crisp styles of Rebula offer the most occasions for consumers to open a bottle, when they just want good quality, enjoyable wine at a fair price. Then come the impressive, complex, oaked styles, sometimes with skin contact and age. The best are amazing wines that can build prestige (and win those top international medals). These are "big wines for big glasses" on special occasions and in top restaurants. Then Rebula can deliver endless fascination in a multitude of other styles, from vibrant sparkling to luscious, sweet versions, as well as stunning amber and amphora wines. So Rebula can genuinely offer something for everyone.

This book brings together some of these threads, exploring how and why is the grape has survived on the rocky terraces of the Brda region and has even today built something of a global reputation. This is largely thanks to the vision of one man - Zvonimir "Miro" Simčič – and thanks to the in-depth research by the author, Noah Charney, you can read his story with a glass of Rebula in hand.

- Dr Caroline Gilby MW

1

TO SPIT
OR TO
SWALLOW:
A NOVICE
AT THE
MASTERCLASS

TO SPIT OR TO SWALLOW: A NOVICE AT THE MASTERCLASS

To spit or to swallow? That became the question just a few minutes in to my first proper wine tasting. There I was, seated along with 75 members of the international wine community, from the editor of a major wine magazine to critics and sommeliers from the United States to Tokyo and numerous countries in between. We sat in a grand Renaissance hall at Vila Vipolže, just on the Slovenian side of the Italian border. The theme was a very special wine, indigenous to this region, called Rebula. As an American writer and professor living, for the last decade, in Slovenia, I am intrigued by all that is local. My inner art historian makes me want to research the stories behind traditions, to engage with the culture as deeply as I can, and to ask questions that might not occur to locals, since they are used to things that I see as rare, exotic treasures.

Now, let it be known that, while I have occasionally written about wine, I am no expert. I am an enthusiastic amateur who does not really know the difference between a Bordeaux and Burgundy. This wine tasting thing was all new to me, but I was keen to participate in an event that would allow me to taste the Rebula wines produced by 15 local vintners, many of whom are at the very highest level internationally and one of whose Rebula wines received a rating of 100 out of 100 from a prominent Italian wine critic. That wine has not been openly for sale, and this was a rare chance to taste it. This was an opportunity not to miss.

I felt increasingly uncertain as I approached the event. I knew that I could not drink everything we would be served because, for various reasons, it is considered improper etiquette to be drunk off your ass at a formal wine tasting. On the other hand, I find spitting mildly repulsive. The setting was glamorous, elegant, and sophisticated, and I didn't want to make a fool of myself. Which is why I looked confusedly and indecisively at the black spittoon perched between my seat and that of my neighbor at the tasting, a wine maker from Chile who had flown in especially for this event. Thankfully this spittoon came equipped with a cover, but it nevertheless felt very strange to be in such an elegant, formal atmosphere...and have everyone around me hocking loogies into a black bucket. Spitting and elegant etiquette seem diametrically opposed, and yet that is the essence of wine tastings. Sip, swish, spit...then invent elaborate metaphors for what you just tasted ("oaky yet pedantic, with an aftertaste of burnt orange peel and chewy marshmallow pillowcases").

Make no mistake, Slovenia is a major international wine producer in quality, if not in scale. Gašper Čarman, Slovenia's resident wine guru, considers the hills of Goriška Brda to be one of

Vila Vipolže

Masterclass – Brda, home of rebula, Vila Vipolže

the top five terroirs in the world for wine growing. Igor Simčič (father of Simon Simčič, who we'll meet shortly), of Medot Winery, echoed the sentiment, saying, "You have to try very hard to make a bad wine here." Provided you steer clear of *cviček* (which, though I do appreciate the local cultural tradition of drinking it, should not be classified in the same category), Slovenian wines can punch with the best of them. I always prefer indigenous specialties, and so the chance to taste Rebula, a grape with a rich history dating back to the Middle Ages but specialized to the border area between Slovenia and Italy, is as good a wine tasting as the world can offer.

There were 15 wines to taste. I tried to spit. Really, I did. But here's the thing: if you don't provide some propulsion when you spit, which inevitably involves making that guttural hocking sound, then instead of spitting you sort of drool. Very unsophisticated. Nor is it sophisticated to make guttural hocking sounds and propel the expelled wine into the spittoon. I clearly needed more practice to strike a balance. I found the whole thing pretty repulsive and also felt that I was so concerned with the spitting part that I wasn't tasting the wine properly.

So, I sipped and swallowed and realized very quickly that I had not eaten a big enough breakfast to last through the tasting. I ended with a compromise. I took miniature, doll-sized sips of wine. I didn't have to spit, and I didn't get hammered. Just lightly toasted. It seemed to me like Ms. Manners would be okay with this.

And the wines were so good. My initial concern was that I knew so little about wine that maybe I wouldn't even be able to distinguish one from another, the good from the less good (I foolishly assumed that nothing actively bad would be included). Turns out that you don't need a black belt in wine to spot the good stuff. Without naming names, 2 of the wines were un-drinkably dreadful. I noted that the Italian wine expert leading the tasting used a euphemism—iodine—to describe the scent and, heaven help us, the taste of them both. Iodine, it turns out, is a wine world euphemism for wine that smells and tastes like licking the floor of a men's toilet. In my notes for the two terrible wines, I see that I wrote (in a nearly indecipherable, alcohol-induced scrawl) "strange toilet-y scent" followed by "nothing to like" and "I'm no fan of an 'iodine trace' or 'pine resin hints.'" The other was a "natural wine" about which I wrote "nose inside the urinal now, Jesus Christ!" Natural wine is a lovely idea—you harvest the grapes, store and ferment them, and let nature do what it will, adding nothing. The only problem is that ideology can trump end result, and many natural wines, while natural, are naturally undrinkable. But the good wines were excellent, even transcendental. I adored everything I tasted from someone with the surname Simčič. That's Simon, Edi, and Marjan, none of them related, it turns out (there are loads of Simčičes running around the region). The Medot Rebula Journey 2018 from Simon's vineyard had "a rose nose, pallid fruit, fresh, salty capers" thing going on. Of Edi's Rebula Fojana 2017 I wrote "buttered toast nose, butter on toast to taste…butter on my nose…so rich, I can't stop drinking it." Of Marjan's 100-point Rebula Opoka 2016 Medana Jama Cru, I got all poetic: "echoing mineral cavern taste, buttered ginger apricots, orange zest scent, tangy ending." At least, that's what I think I wrote. There was definitely butter involved, but the script is so wonky that I might've written "opening mouthful caustic tank, buttocks gingerly apple tarts, orangutan test cents, thongy bending." But the most mind-bending was the Gravner Ribolla 2011, a copper color, "old cork scent," that was more like whiskey than wine, like a "liquefied old leather wallet…peppery, heavy Indian spices, tobacco, single malt whiskey" and "long legs" (which I think means a lot of tannins but could just have been me describing my own legs, as this was the 15th glass consumed on an empty stomach).

What I came away with was a great appreciation for this grape variety and the desire to learn more. About the region, about local wine-making traditions, about the vintners, about Slovenia and Italy's liquid gold. And so, since I am a professor and used to researching, I dug deeper and started drinking more heavily (but also more thoughtfully). Everywhere I went, everyone I asked, about the story of wine in this spectacular slice of terroir along the Slovenian-Italian border, the more I heard a single name, the godfather of it all: Zvonimir (Miro) Simčič.

World-renowned wine critics and journalists networking at Masterclass

2
IN
(S)LOVE
WITH
SLOVENIA

IN (S)LOVE WITH SLOVENIA

Back in 2000, as an American student studying in London, I embarked on a "Eurorail" trip. Such a holiday is a rite of passage among American students, almost de rigeur. It functions as a sort of smorgasbord of European cities. You purchase an open ticket that allows you to travel indefinitely by train throughout Europe. Backpack loaded (and possibly emblazoned with a Canadian flag, because sometimes we Americans masquerade as universally beloved Canadians, when travelling abroad), you then hop on and off the trains as much as you like, exploring one city after another. Fancy a day in Lisbon? Two in Copenhagen? Off you go. To make your wallet stretch further, you can even board trains in the evening, sleep during the journey, and wake in a new city, eliminating the need to spring for a hostel bed.

Prior to my own Eurorailing adventure, I lent my *Lonely Planet: Europe on a Shoestring* to five friends who had already been on such a trip, asking them for notes, suggestions, annotations. All five, without colluding, told me that Slovenia's Lake Bled was the single most beautiful place they had seen in all of Europe.

Fast-forward to 2006, when I was a postgraduate student, and I wound up embarking on a longer-form, 'slow food' version of my train travel smorgasbord. I would live in eight different European cities, each for at least a month, to get a feel for what it would be like to move there indefinitely. With forays into Venice, Florence, Rome, Madrid, Leiden and more, I ended up in Ljubljana. And that is where I fell in love—with the country and with the current (and future) Mrs. Charney.

And this is what I fell in love with.

In order to marry her, on our wedding day, I was obliged to survive the dreaded "shranga," a gauntlet of pre-nuptial feats of manliness required of aspiring grooms from beyond the Slovenian mountain village confines, if they wish to marry a local girl. Once I got through the admittedly nerve-racking bouts of scythe-sharpening, bark-shaving, axe-wielding, and, yes, even wife-buying traditions, and was permitted by the grumpy-looking villagers to enter the church and carry on with my matrimony, I felt that this was the place for me and I have come to feel truly a part of it.

Slovenia has been, for me, a land of opportunity. I may be a best-selling, Pulitzer-nominated author but I'm also practically the only Anglophone writer in this country of two million. This means the pickings may be slim when it comes to collaborations with foreign writers, but it's

The typical terroir of the region

been my delight to be those pickings. I'm regularly invited to participate in wonderfully exciting projects with fascinating, brilliant Slovenes. And I'm certainly the most active foreigner in Slovenia when it comes to media appearances. This has meant that I've become something of Slovenia's foreign "cheerleader," eager to tell travelers and potential expats of the wonders of this little nation. I even published a book, *Slovenology: Living and Traveling in the World's Best Country,* which is part memoir, part to travelogue, and part essay collection singing its praises.

There are only so many times that Slovenia can be called a "hidden gem" and still claim to remain hidden. But those who come to this tiny country nestled between the Alps and the Adriatic inevitably seem to feel that they've discovered a little-known paradise. While cheap flights from London have made it an easy weekend destination, and the capital of Ljubljana is popular on the stag and hen party circuits, the entire country is a wonderland landscape. Beyond the confines of charming, Zürich-like Ljubljana, Slovenia offers travelers a destination that is at once easy to navigate (with English spoken at a high level just about everywhere you go), one of the safest countries in the world, not to mention the cleanest (National Geographic's 2017 World Legacy Award winner as the most sustainable tourist destination, and Ljubljana was Green Capital of Europe in 2016).

But that's what the guidebooks will tell you. Having chosen this country as my new homeland, settling in the charming three-castled alpine town of Kamnik, just north of the capital, I wanted to get to know it in a deeper, and more intimate way. I wanted a local's-eye-view of the secret facets of this "hidden gem." And so I hatched a plan.

I set about, in a calculated way, contacting people I admired or found interesting—for instance, the great folk-rock musician, Vlado Kreslin, and the world-famous chef, Janez Bratovž, and the expat Bosnian actor and director, Branko Djurić—and requested an interview. To my delight, everyone acquiesced. In Slovenia, everyone writes their own email, and even the prime minister is just a message away. I struck up friendships and collaborations with many of the people I met in this way, working my way through a who's-who of interesting Slovenians.

I wrote to Bratovž, known to all as JB, to interview him for an article I prepared for a food magazine, asking the question of whether great chefs should also be considered great artists. It seemed to be a question that chefs were intrigued to answer. I was surprised to be given interviews with Éric Ripert and Ferran Adrià, among a dozen others. From Slovenia, I spoke to

Ana Roš, world female chef of the year in 2017, and JB. It turned out that JB lives near me, in Kamnik, and we went for a beer. We hit it off and decided on a convenient excuse to continue drinking beer together: writing a cookbook.

JB has been rated the tenth-best chef in Europe and is the godfather of nouvelle cuisine in the former Yugoslavia—the first to introduce carpaccio and rare steak to a land of delicious but well-done cutlets smothered in cream sauces. JB picked twenty key ingredients that he uses in his cooking and, together with photographer Matjaž Tančič, we spent the summer crisscrossing the country, visiting JB's picks for the finest producers of these ingredients.

Steps from the border with Italy, in Goriška Brda, we tasted what many think is the world's best prosciutto, or *pršut* (pronounced "per-shoot") in Slovenian. Just eighty legs a year from indigenous, wonderfully fatty Blackstrap pigs are lovingly prepared by Uroš Klinec and pre-sold to select restaurants around the globe. From the Caravaggesque darkness of his cellar, a vegetarian's nightmare (but this carnivore's delight) of hanging hocks of ham, we emerged onto his sun-soaked patio, overlooking the wine-rich hills, and tasted prosciutto so delicate and light that it melts on the tongue, requiring no use of teeth to consume. Across the country, in the Prekmurje flatlands, we tasted the finest Styrian pumpkin seed oil, hand-pressed in century-old presses by the Kocbek family, and of such flavor and delicacy that it is used not only to dress salads, but as a sauce for ice cream and to lace dark chocolate bars. We wound serpentine through the hills of Tolmin, above the emerald Soča River, a real-life Narnia (one of the franchise movies was even filmed here), to meet a farm bringing back the colossal, leopard skinned Soča River trout, with flesh so delicious and delicate that today it is only served as a carpaccio. This king of trout nearly went extinct due to overfishing in the First World War, with hungry soldiers flinging grenades into the river to catch a meal. At the ancient salt flats near Piran, on Slovenia's dollhouse-sized 46 km of karstic coast, we met Dario, whose family has been harvesting salt for generations, from flats that date back to the Roman Empire—when salt was used as pay (the term "salary" comes from *salaria,* meaning "salt"). We drove up a mountain with a mountain-sized sheep farmer eager to show us his dominion, arriving at the top only to find the still-warm remains of gutted sheep, which showed that a bear was lurking somewhere nearby in the darkness barely held back by the ebbing twilight (I opted to stay in the car for that one, while Tančič took photographs of the farmer and JB smoked and

A fantastic view of Dobrovo Castle as seen from a Rebula vineyard

kept an eye out for bears and wolves). We dipped down to the Istrian peninsula to meet a former real estate lawyer, Aleš Winkler. He sold his fancy Ljubljana apartment, bought thirty goats as lawnmowers for his rural holiday house, taught himself to make goat cheese online and, within a year, was the goat cheese champion of Croatia—and this year gave the keynote speech for Slow Food International, teaching Italians and French how to make a proper *chevre*. Upon the vast, verdant meadow atop a mesa-like alpine mountain, Velika Planina, dotted with odd, low-slung shepherds' huts that recall The Shire and are marked by highly localized traditions (including a rain-repelling shepherds' gown made of strips of shaven tree and anti-witch knives carved with runes), we sampled breast-shaped cheese, Trnič (which always comes in pairs).

That summer's travels with JB opened up locations and delicacies that I'd never have found on my own, and for which I am most grateful, for they allowed a constellation of indigenous ingredients to show me an intimate, insider's portrait of my adopted country—and they led to a cookbook called *Slovenian Cuisine: From the Alps to the Adriatic in 20 Ingredients*.

Part of this foodie road trip included a visit to Goriška Brda for that crazy good *pršut*. This landscape of rolling hills and vineyards haunted me. While there, I also tasted a wine I'd never heard of before, but loved straight away: Rebula or, as it's known just a stone's throw across the border in Italy, Ribolla Gialla.

I am fascinated by places, people, and foods and how those three components meet to create singular experiences, whether today or historically. Rebula, yes, Goriška Brda yes, but also Tito: the president of Yugoslavia from 1943-1980 is one of the very few historical figures from this part of the world known to all Americans. Years ago, I helped edit the English translation of a brick-thick biography of Tito, and I recall a reference to his favorite wine. Rebula was the crème de la crème for Yugoslav state events and now, invited to participate in the Rebula Masterclass, I was able to taste it for the first time. In that room full of people who were, well, actually qualified to write about wine, I was struck by the union of some names that I kept hearing: Rebula, Goriška Brda, Tito and a confusingly long list of prominent winemakers with the surname Simčič. But one Simčič was mentioned at seemingly every turn, by just about every winemaker I spoke to, and certainly in every lecture and speech given at that Masterclass: Zvonimir.

I was so intrigued that I decided to write this book. To tell the story of the region, the wine, and the man who wove the two together. I do all this from the perspective of a double outsider: as a foreigner in love with this hidden gem of a country and its myriad facets and as a foreigner to a deep understanding of wine. Other than knowing how to write a story well, I'm thoroughly unqualified, which makes me just the sort of narrator that I like to read. Texts by experts for experts tend to be dry, and experts writing well for the general public are a rare breed. I enjoy the "gonzo" travelogues of someone with an open mind and adventurous spirit throwing themselves into things they know little about and the reader (or viewer, as I also occasionally host television programs) gets to learn along with them. So that's where we are here: a wine book written by someone who likes wine but who thought that Chateau Lafitte is French for "castle of the feet."

My process of learning about the area mirrors my learning about wine. For wine experts, then, this exploration of a unique grape variety will offer some insights and a definitive guide with everything except the expert tasting notes. For oenophiles who aren't oenologists—me included—then join for the wild ride through geography, history, food, fascinating biography, and, of course, a whole lot of wine tastings.

Rebula: where destinies intertwine

3
THE MAN
BEHIND
THE GOLD
WINE

THE MAN BEHIND THE GOLD WINE

Yugoslavia knew how to party. The Anglophone world has a skewed view of this part of the world. For most, life in Yugoslavia was nothing like the old videos of bread lines in the Communist USSR. It was the world's most successful experiment in socialism and, while it didn't work out in the end, the quality of life was quite high, the joie de vivre at reasonable levels, and the appreciation of the finer things in life—laughter, friendship, schnapps, and wine—was a shared trait from Serbia to Slovenia, from Croatia to Macedonia, from Bosnia to Montenegro. And of all the wines produced in the former Yugoslavia, there was one that was the favorite, whether you asked the political power players in Belgrade or a group of villagers. "The golden one," they called it. "Rebula."

There is ample evidence that Rebula was a favorite wine among the elite of former Yugoslavia (before that assemblage of nations dissolved and Slovenia became independent, in 1991), folks who could buy foreign wines if they wanted to, but who recognized that their own country produced wine at the highest level internationally. An archive of a list of delicacies ordered for state dinners enumerates all manner of luxury ingredients, and a number of wines, but Rebula is in the lead.

"The golden one" was a good choice for several reasons, the taste but one among them. The wine is made from Rebula grapes, which are indigenous to the region that now straddles the border between Italy and Slovenia. On the Italian side the area is called Collio, in Slovenia it is Goriška Brda. The terroir is the same, and it is a region that has been rated by experts as among the top five wine terroirs on the planet, right up there with Bordeaux and Tuscany, and other more storied geographies. Andrew Jefford called Rebula "a dream wine of a new age." Caroline Gilby wrote that while "international grapes can be great here, but it's Rebula that can really put Slovenia on the map." *Wine Spectator's* Robert Camuto joked that the only "problem" facing the Goriška Brda/Collio region was that "in such a small territory, so many wines excel." Thus, Rebula wine could be considered by Yugoslav leaders to be a Yugoslav specialty, and one of the highest levels of quality—ideal for showcasing the best of what their nation could produce, when entertaining foreign dignitaries.

That Rebula was cultivated in Yugoslavia, that the world knows of Rebula, and that Rebula wine continues to be, and ever more-so, considered among the world's finest wines (including winning gold and platinum medals from *Decanter* magazine and being named the world's best wine by the 2010 world's best sommelier, Luca Gardini), is thanks to one visionary man. The "godfather of Rebula," as he is known, could easily be dubbed the godfather of Goriška Brda, or even, as my experience indicated, the godfather of Slovenian wine. Under his inspiration and leadership, Goriška Brda transformed from a lovely but impoverished cluster of villages into one of the globe's great wine producers, providing a substantial, high-end industry that employed an improbably high percentage of its residents. This, in turn, put Slovenian wine on the world map. Throughout a decades-long ascent, this man championed an ancient, but humble and out-of-favor, hyper-local grape. He focused on microclimate and "zero kilometer" local produce, half a century before it was à la mode. He is an example of how one person's passion, drive, commitment, and inherent elegance can transform a product, a region, a nation for the better.

His name was Zvonimir or, as his friends called him, Miro.

* * * * *

Miro slips on a heavy, patterned gray cardigan as he enters the mineral cool of the dark cellars. A cardigan that has not been in style for more than a decade, but no matter. It only adds to the charm of the man who wears it. His hands conduct the air above row upon row of dark glass bottles, many cloaked in dust. His archive wines. He sits at a stone table inside the cellar, beside an illuminated candle. There is something timeless, ritualistic, even monastic about his actions and goals, as he continues a tradition that dates back more than a millennium, when the 13th-century monks of the nearby Abbazia di Rosazzo tended to their Rebula vines and sampled the resulting wine in a similar setting. He sips his wine in a particular way. The glass stem is supported by his pointer and middle fingers in front and his ring and pinkie finger behind, the ring finger tucked back, balancing the flute with a practiced geometry.

Here is a man who saw the world through rose-tinted glasses, and not just metaphorically. Sure, he is a positive soul, always seeing the best, most optimized route forward in any given situation, solving any given problem. But he *does* wear rose-tinged sunglasses to protect those focused eyes from the glare of the warming sun, as it floods down upon his rows of vines, pouring sweetness into them. He tends those vines with patience and grandfatherly affection. There he stands, clasping his left hand inside his right, against the backdrop of a princely estate, sundrenched and endlessly picturesque. But this gentleman vintner trims his grapes while wearing the blue overall jacket of socialist workers. This balance of elegance and sophistication with a feeling for honest, humble hard work is a mark of the man. His white hair is combed upwards on either side of his head, cresting like a wave above his brow. He lived in a time when the socialist environment did not encourage thinking outside the box. That makes his vision, drive and passion, his fearlessness, his willingness to stand out and stand up for his passions, so much more impressive.

Zvonimir Simčič, Miro to his friends, was a member of the Ordo Equestris Vini Europae (the European Knights of Wine Order), but his chivalric manner and persona were self-evident without the need for heraldic attire. His firm, proper kindness and humble elegance were in-built, and he is rightfully admired and praised throughout the world of fine wines. He is considered the godfather of Rebula, an ancient grape indigenous to the borderlands between Italy and Slovenia, the heart of which is his native Goriška Brda. Miro championed this hyper-local variety at a time when it was not the done thing. His peers and the authorities wanted to rip out the Rebula vines and plant international varieties of the sort that sold well abroad, for which there was a constant demand: Merlot, Cabernet, Chardonnay. But Miro held fast to his principles, to the benefits of locality, decades before the concept of zero-kilometer consumption or "locavores" had been established. He believed in the indigenous, historically relevant grape of his homeland, a grape so storied that it was mentioned by the leading writer on agriculture of ancient Rome, Lucius Junius Moderatus Columella. Rebula was the favorite white variety among aristocrats in the region during the Middle Ages and valued at the highest rate among wines under the 18th-century reign of Empress Maria Theresa—we know this because, in 1751, she introduced a new taxation system, which taxed Rebula higher than any wine, red or white, throughout the Habsburg dominion. Rebula nevertheless fell into limited use in the first half of the 20th century. It was Miro who focused on bringing it back to the fore, recognizing in it a rare white that has the complexity of a red and can be treated in an array of variations. Miro was a pioneer of this sparkling incarnation in the 1960s, establishing Rebula as a serious, award-winning wine on the international map, paving the way for the handful of leading producers in the region, on either side of the Slovenian-Italian border, who continue to

Zvonimir Simčič, Medot

wow the critics with Rebula wines, from still to sparkling, from dry to sweet, from steel-aged to barrique.

Most of us will not be known for any great legacy after we pass on. Most of us will have simply lived. Perhaps we have given birth to a new generation. Hopefully we have lived a life of love and warmth. But with our passing, only our families and friends will remember us, and only those who actually knew us in person.

But certain people have a greatness about them. They are part of historically important moments, decisions, actions. Some even start revolutions, be they large or small, violent or silent. Miro is one such person. He is a sort of godfather to winemakers of the region beyond the confines of his family, and a name held in esteem by in-the-know wine lovers. He will always be remembered in history books, in wine lore, and beyond. He forged a number of legacies that endure and thrive thanks to his ingenuity, drive, perfectionism, and vision.

- It is thanks to the movement that Miro began that Goriška Brda rose from an impoverished region to a noble, high-end destination for tourism and agriculture, thanks to its international standing as one of the world's great wine terroirs.

- That Klet Brda produced wine of the highest quality that became known as Golden Rebula, receiving international critical recognition, for he ran Klet Brda from its establishment until his retirement.

- That Klet Brda introduced, for the first time, sparkling Rebula made in Charmat tanks— the easier method, employed for most Prosecco. This was marketed as Sparkling Rebula.

- That Klet Brda features only locally-grown grapes, preserving the brilliance of the terroir— administrators wanted the winery to be a catch-all for grapes of multiple regions, which would have ruined the individuality and quality of its products.

- That Klet Brda, the most important winery in Slovenia (and, when it was founded, in Yugoslavia), was established in 1957 in Goriška Brda. It was a co-op that became the region's primary industry, and remains so, producing over 4 million bottles a year, uniting 400 local families and 1000 hectares of vines, and selling in 26 countries.

· That his personal, family winery, Medot, is considered a pioneer among the region's best for sparkling wines made using the same methods as in Champagne based on Rebula, for he decanted the knowledge he developed studying and running Klet Brda into Medot, the passion project of his very active retirement.

· And it is thanks to Miro that the hyper-local white grape variety, Rebula, indigenous to this small slice of the planet, has received international recognition and praise. For he insisted that the mighty Klet Brda focus on Rebula, when the powers-that-be wanted to grow foreign varieties.

He brought Rebula, almost single-handedly, back from a historical footnote into modern prominence. In this way, he foreshadowed the current movement for microclimates, hyper-locality, zero-kilometer production (using goods that come from less than a kilometer away from where they will be processed), and pride in indigenous ingredients.

Miro is synonymous with Goriška Brda, Klet Brda, Medot, and Rebula.

And this is the story of the man and his legacy.

4

MIRO
AND
KLET
BRDA

MIRO AND KLET BRDA

I know nothing about wine.

How's that for an encouraging way to kick off a wine book? Nothing like soothing the reader with the assurance that they're in good hands. Well, I started this project knowing next to nothing about wine. But now, with my research complete and in the process of writing it, I know a lot, particularly about Rebula and winemaking along the Slovenia/Italy border. My journey will become yours. I know all about how to research and write about complex ideas in an engaging, clear way. So my approach to this project is to assume I know nothing and try to absorb (and imbibe) as much as possible along the way.

With extensive experience writing for magazines and newspapers and in writing biography, I approach research by first asking for interviews. In order for me to get to know Miro, I need to speak with those who knew him. I was grateful that everyone I asked, including such heavy hitters as the first president of Slovenia, eagerly volunteered. So in diving into this triple biography of a book—about the person, Miro, the place, Goriška Brda, and the wine, Rebula—I spent a great deal of time exploring, imbibing, and interviewing.

Miro left numerous legacies that can still be felt today. The one that comes across most palpably is the respect for him and love of him that shines in the eyes of each person I ask to share their memories of him. Italian, Slovenian, or other, all agree that he was a gentleman through and through. Being a good person seems to be the best of all possible legacies, but if you're looking for the sort that end up in the history books, he checks many such boxes as well. As we have seen, he is the man most responsible for the transformation of Goriška Brda from impoverished hinterland to world wine destination. He established and led Klet Brda, Yugoslavia's largest and most prestigious winery. He introduced champagne techniques to make sparkling Rebula. He resurrected Rebula as a variety and made it a global star. Miro's quest was not about personal enrichment—it was about helping to pull up his home region from a situation of truly abject poverty, and the only way he could conceive of doing so was through wine.

Miro's son, Igor Simčič, explained it to me: "It's important to know that our territory, before the First World War, was part of the Austro-Hungarian Empire. It was a region known for fruit and wine as far away as Vienna. After the First World War, this region was suddenly part of Italy. And all of that northern market for products from this region disappeared. After the Second World War, the southern markets were cut off, and we were no longer able to trade with

Italy, which we had grown used to over the decades between the wars. We were part of Yugoslavia. But between the wars and even into the early 1960s, Goriška Brda was a place of extreme poverty. Sometimes we even lacked drinking water. There was no electricity. People struggled, died. I remember, as a child of six or so, when I would come to visit my grandparents, every little scrap of food was important. My father grew up with this poverty and was determined to do everything he could to make his homeland, the land of his parents, live better. He saw wine as the only solution, as this was a region of wine."

In order to take the first step on this benevolent crusade, Miro had to first educate himself, as winemaking in the region was old-fashioned and stagnant. Igor continues, "He went off to the best academy for wine, at Conegliano—it is still among the best in the world today—with this mission in mind. To use wine to help pull his home region out of poverty. There he came into contact with world-class experts and state-of-the-art knowledge. That knowledge came home with him and passed on what he learned. He maintained regular contact with this academy, and so was always aware of the cutting edge of wine technology and advances."

Even armed with the best of contemporary knowledge on winemaking, Miro faced an uphill battle. On the one hand, locals were hard-wired to continue what they were used to and required convincing to introduce novel techniques. Igor described the old habits to me. ""From his youth, my father was determined to help his home region financially through wine. The region would not go anywhere without technological advancement. The regime of the time, the Socialist government, had a plan in mind to build a nationalized wine cellar in Nova Gorica, the nearest larger city. They would drive grapes grown in both Goriška Brda and the Vipava Valley to Nova Gorica to be processed and made into wine. The officials were not familiar with the various technical processes involved, and if they had forced this plan through, it would have been a proper catastrophe, from a logistical standpoint but also from the standpoint of mixing grapes from two distinct terroirs of rich potential into one conglomerate, mass-produced set of wines. But the officials over in Ljubljana had faith in my father and took his advice. He argued that the only way forward was to create two separate, smaller cellars, one in Vipava and one in Brda, because they were two neighboring but entirely different terroirs. This was at a time several decades before the concept of terroirs was commonplace, of course. To mix grapes from the two regions would be like mixing apples and pears and selling a fruit juice, instead of a top-quality apple juice and a top-quality pear juice, separately."

Convincing locals was one thing, but there was also a socialist regime to navigate. Yugoslavia was a political entity that did not support independent innovation. "These decisions were made centrally and were often not deeply thought-out," Igor continues. "Those deciding were remotely located, were rarely experts, and often had other interests. But Miro took this really personally, because it was about defending his home. And he was one of the only people in Yugoslavia at the time who had this specialized knowledge from a foreign wine academy. He knew how to argue in a convincing manner, and also how to navigate the egos and politics of the Yugoslav system. He convinced the powers-that-be that this was the only solution."

Establishing businesses and doing something out of the ordinary required governmental approval. "It was absolutely more difficult for him," Igor confirms, "because he always remained politically neutral. The idea that you could be in an elevated position, as director of a leading wine cellar, without being a member of the Communist Party, was basically unthinkable. But he had an elegant solution to this concern, too. They called him once to explain that he could not be director if he were not in the Party, that he must be an exemplar to those who work for him and his community... And he replied, 'Look, I'll do it however you like, but I'll tell you this: I cannot work two positions at once. I can either be a businessman for you, or a politician. It's up to you. I'll do what you say.' In this way, he neutralized their concerns, and someone in the administration decided, 'Let's leave him to work at the cellar. At least that way we'll be sure to drink good wine at all the endless meetings we have to go to.'"

Thus Miro, with the skill of a general, managed at least three fronts: working with locals and convincing them that his avant-garde approach was the best for Goriška Brda, keeping tabs on the cutting edge of wine throughout the world to know the level Brda wines had to reach to establish themselves, and handling the rigid Yugoslav politics. The indigenous grape, Rebula, was central to all three fronts.

"There were two key decisions that he made on behalf of his territory," Igor concludes. "The first was that he convinced the local authorities to build a coop wine cellar, *Klet Brda,* for the region, and a second one in the nearby Vipava Valley. He was responsible for the technical side of this project, along with Professor Veselič. The second important decision was that he would

Zvonimir Simčič supervising the building of the new winery in Brda, 1957

make Rebula the focal wine variety for the region when deciding what to plant. When the authorities in Ljubljana learned of this choice of Rebula, they phoned him up and said, 'Have you gone mad? No one knows Rebula. You should be planting Chardonnay or Pinot!' And he replied, 'It's true that it's not known. But we are the only ones who have it. Because I believe in the quality of Rebula, it will be our primary grape.'"

5

REBULA:
THE
MAKING
OF THE
GOLD
WINE

REBULA: THE MAKING OF THE GOLD WINE

In order to get to know a wine, the best way is to taste it. With any luck, you've got a bottle on the table beside you, possibly on your bedside table as you read this book (I'm not one to judge), and you can enjoy a sip as you read about the wine's qualities. But on the off chance that a glass of Rebula is not within easy reach, perhaps the next best thing is to ask a handful of experts—winemakers and critics—for their thoughts. I was happy to do this on your behalf—and mine.

Rebula has been featured—and praised—in all the important wine publications. Alessio Turazza, wine critic for Italian wine guide, *Gambero Rosso*, wrote "Rebula is the symbol of the cross-border terroir of Collio-Brda." Robert Camuto, an Italy-based writer for *Wine Spectator*, noted, "This region has only one problem. That in one tiny terroir so many varieties prosper." Giovanni Angelucci, writing for *La Stampa,* called Rebula "a concentrate of history." Caroline Gilby, a contributor to *Decanter* (an author of the Foreword to this book), was effusive: "Whether you call it Rebula or Ribolla Gialla, the flagship grape of Slovenia's Brda region is a bit of a rebel. This shows in the way it hung on here against a tide of international interlopers and in the way it reveals its best when fighting for life on the region's steep slopes and dry, rocky soils. Rebula accounts for one-fifth of the region's vines and is a key part of Brda's identity. About 30% of its hills lie over the border in Italy's Collio vineyards straddling the border. It's really a single region divided by national borders, but politics don't change geography." Wine critic Andrew Jefford called Rebula "Slovenia's dream white. One of the wine dreams of our age is the white which behaves like a red. Which would have, in other words, a structural presence, a texture, a depth and a frame of reference altogether different, and perhaps altogether grander, than the conventional whites we know. You could say that the new dream overlaps at that point with a more familiar one: the search for the 'new Chardonnay.' Not the quest to find a new quasi-universal white variety of almost limitless adaptability, but the quest to find a variety capable, in favored zones, of surrendering white wines which can attain (over an ageing trajectory) the kind of sumptuous, banquet-like complexity of white burgundy. Are these just dreams? Well, that would be enough: we need dreams to carry us forward. But a handful of truly interesting indigenous varieties perfectly adapted to their sites can indeed suggest such a possibility. Somewhere near the top of that short list, for me, comes Rebula. I had a chance to fall in love with it all over again...in Brda."

These are among the wine experts who have fallen in love with Rebula. But most of our time will be spent with *Rebula* experts.

There are varying stories about how Zlata Rebula, Golden Rebula, got to be called "golden." Each person I asked about its origin was equally certain that their version was correct, but the truth seems lost in time. It did win many gold medals at major wine competitions (including ten years in a row at the international wine competition in Ljubljana), and this is one reason it might have received its nickname. It certainly was and is golden in color, thanks to its thicker skin left in longer contact with the juice, so it could be as simple as that. Tito is said to have once described it as "the golden one," so that is another origin story. And it might have been a marketing ploy to garner more respect for it, a tactic inserted by Zvonimir to great success. In fact, all of these origin stories have a ring of truth to them, so perhaps it's like the solution to the whodunnit in Agatha Christie's *Murder on the Orient Express*: the answer to the question of which one is guilty is—all of them.

* * * * *

Miro was also a brilliant defender of branding. Rebula grapes can be grown elsewhere, of course, and there is Rebula wine from the Vipava Valley, a wine region adjacent to Goriška Brda—the main winery there was also designed with Miro's consultation. What distinguishes Brda Rebula from other versions of it is the terroir. When other regions began to promote Rebula wines, Miro rolled up his sleeves and went on the counter-offensive, promoting the Brda terroir and branding. He launched a highly successful campaign with billboards emblazoned with the motto "*Rebula da, ampak ta Briška*," ("Rebula yes, but the one from Goriška Brda"). He also focused on branding Rebula in two quality levels: one was simply Rebula, a very good table wine, but the other was a higher-level Zlata Rebula (Golden Rebula). This association with gold rang true, and this is what likely stuck in Tito's mind when he asked for "the golden one" at that restaurant in Portorož.

I spoke to Vili Mišigoj, long-time secretary of the cooperative winery, Klet Brda, and effectively its second in command while Miro ran it. "All of Yugoslavia received our Rebula. And it was not enough that our Rebula was enjoyed throughout Yugoslavia, in Belgrade and Zagreb, but he added the marketing term 'Golden Rebula.' So he experimented and offered normal Rebula and Golden Rebula. The Golden Rebula was well-received. We don't know exactly how he came up with the term, Golden Rebula, but it was his idea and he developed the label. He also shifted the technique to make it lightly sparkling. It was, of course, called Golden because of its natural color. There's a story that Tito came to Portorož. And his colleagues asked him, 'What sort of wine shall we drink?' Someone suggested, 'We have Rebula from Goriška Brda.' And he replied, 'Yes, but the golden one.' One story goes that this phrase of Tito's established the term. It stuck and we began to sell Golden Rebula. But we don't know which came first, Engineer Simčič's idea or Tito's request for Rebula...but the golden one."

I kept on hearing that this terroir is among the world's best for white wine, and this made me want to know why. Americans like me are drawn to superlatives: the biggest, the best, the first. I'm of a generation of, well, hipster Americans from cities who are likewise fascinated by the hyper-local, by quirky micro-stories that shed light on specific geographical locations to which you must travel to experience. As an art history professor, I enjoy going to universal museums, where I can see scores of masterpieces in one go. That's an equivalent to the Rebula Masterclass, tasting more than a dozen of the best in a single room. But I actually prefer to travel to see a single artwork in some remote castle, chapel, or wayward gallery, to enjoy the journey, the anticipation, the uniqueness of the place, the scent of the room around the work, the look of the custodian as he lets in this over-enthusiastic art historian to see a particular piece, the atmosphere of the land around it, the genius loci of encountering a work in situ, where it was meant to be displayed and where it has "lived" for centuries. This journey-as-quest approach works well with indigenous wine varieties as well as local masterworks of painting or sculpture.

Rebula is, for me, a perfect storm: indigenous, rich in history, and the imbibable embodiment of a beautiful, exotic landscape to which one must pilgrimage.

But I know art history inside and out. When I travel to Koper, Slovenia to see the Carpaccio altarpiece, or to Volterra, Italy to see the *Deposition* by Rosso Fiorentino, or to the hospital on the outskirts of Dijon, France to see Claus Sluter's monumental sculpture, *The Well of Moses,* I feel confident in my foundation in the field that will allow me to understand the artwork I encounter.

This is not at all the case with wine. I'm an enthusiast with no training at all, but with appreciation, energy, thirst to learn, and good will in abundance. So part of my quest was to learn

Rebula/Ribolla Gialla ripening in the Brda/Collio region, overlooking both the Alps and the Mediterranean Sea

Each Rebula/Ribolla Gialla grape is handpicked in this region

as much as I could about Rebula, which meant learning about wine and about Goriška Brda and about the people behind the scenes: Miro, of course, but also the story's contemporary protagonists.

I had to start with the basics. For starters, I realized that I wasn't entirely sure I knew what "terroir" actually meant, so it's best to start at the beginning. Terroir, the French word for "territory," refers to all of the elements that affect how produce grows in a particular area: the quality and constitution of the soil, the topography, the biodiversity of flora and fauna, the climate, and the unique characteristics of the landscape. Everything that nature provides prior to human intervention into agriculture. We've already mentioned the unusual climate, sandwiched between the warm Adriatic and the cool Alps, and that topography of rolling terraced hills. But what gets winemakers most excited about Goriška Brda is the soil. The sum of the aspects of the terroir, coupled with the local agricultural and wine-making traditions, results in a product that is unique to that area, and which will differ from the same wine type made in another terroir.

This was always one of Miro's key arguments in favor of focusing on Rebula, even when the market was clamoring for Cabernet, Merlot, and Chardonnay. Whatever is hyper-local will always be better, more authentic, better suited to the terroir than anything imported.

This book seeks to pay homage to both Brda (Slovenia) and Collio (Italy), which are truly a continued, single terroir divided by a border through the whims of bureaucracy. But data from this chapter, as with most of the book, comes from the Slovenian side. This is simply a logistical matter—I live in Slovenia and worked with a Slovenian team on the book, but the parameters of the terrain and statistics for Collio are similar.

In order to learn, I had to go to the place and learn what I could from the experts. I began with Denis Rusjan, Slovenia's leading wine scientist and a professor of agronomy at the University of Ljubljana. With bright, kind, insightful eyes and a rakish beard, he could be mistaken for a hipster, but balances his youthful aesthetic with scores of high-end publications on the hard science of grapes and soil. His specialization is on flysch geography in Slovenia, so he is the man to speak with. Even if some of my questions might be on the amateur, I-should-really-know-already side of things. He's very kind and, it turns out, some of my silly questions turned out to be intriguing and lead to portals of discovery. He'd given a talk at the Masterclass

I attended, and we met several times to discuss the aspects of the story of Rebula that I know least about: I'm good with history, but anything scientific is often beyond me. But the mark of a mature mind is knowing when to ask for assistance, and I've been lucky enough to find the leading specialists.

Rusjan began by talking about the constitution of the terroir. "The terroir is a combination of local ecology, especially the soil and climate. Brda's soil is heavily mineral and is flysch. The soil here is less rich and fertile because it contains less organic matter. This is in the upper levels of the ground. The topography is also special, in that it consists of small hills, built up at the foot of the Alps millions of years ago. Tectonic movement results in three levels of topography in Brda, aligned from northeast towards the southwest, and this allows morning sun to linger until the late afternoon, so it is sunny from all sides."

What makes the soil great is the double whammy of this having once been beneath a prehistoric ocean (resulting in the high mineral content of the soil), and that the terrain is pocked with small hills. The soil here is called opoka, a special version of flysch—sedimentary rock packed with layers of sandstone and shale. In the local Italian dialect, it is called *ponca*. Organic material runs down those hills when it rains and so, over thousands of years (and really going back millions), organic material would baste the slopes but gather only in the ravines between them. The hills themselves are not very fertile, as that organic material ran off down their slopes. This means that vines grow slowly and sparsely. A novice like me might think this was a bad thing, but not so. What does grow is packed with goodness and of the utmost quality. The "poverty" of the soil makes vines "suffer," as most of the wine experts I spoke to described it, using the exact same word, and this makes their fruit far better and more sophisticated.

Rusjan continues, "Opoka is flysch, a mix of *lapor* (marl), *peščenjak* (sandstone), and other materials. Over millions of years, organic matter would mount up on the surface layers of soil. But because of the hilly nature of Brda, rainfall would wash the organic matter down the hills, leaving the slopes relatively barren of organic material. Organic material decomposed is what provides for fertile soil, so this was absent. Because mechanical farming equipment was not available in the past (today we could move fertile soil to barren spots and compensate for it), this was among the poorer, less fertile areas. The key was the limited amount of organic matter

Opoka in Slovenian or ponca in local Italian dialect - heavily mineral, flysch soil typical of the Brda/Collio terroir, is the signature of the region and accounts for the distinctive taste of Rebula/Ribolla Gialla wine

Organic mass retains water in the soil and releases fertilizer in the form of decomposed material. This poorer soil means that vines grow more slowly, and the flavor of the grapes is more concentrated."

The poor soil is counterbalanced by idyllic climate above-ground. Goriška Brda enjoys plenty of sun, freshness from the sea without interference from its salt-licked winds (it's about 40 km to the Adriatic), and the cool air sweeping down from the Alps. This sums up to slow-growing grapes in no exceptional quantity, but each grape is choice. The famous Burja (Bora) wind is a key factor in this part of the world, as Rusjan explains: "All natural phenomena affect vines. Burja dries out the surface of the earth. It can also break vines and injure grapes. However, wind that blows but does not damage the plants themselves is very welcome, because it dries out the leaves and the drier atmosphere is less conducive to disease. This is what wind does in Brda most of the time."

A drier climate is better? That may seem obvious to oenologists, but Rusjan blew my mind when he pointed out that you've never heard of great wine coming from a jungle climate. Jungles have the most organic matter in the soil, making the soil rich. There is heavy rain so plants grow to incredible sizes and rapidly. This can result in very big grapes, but their size is mostly down to water. They make lousy wine. The best grapes for wine are like the best methods for cooking barbecue: low and slow. Slow growth, plants that have to work hard to extract nutrients from the soil, result in small grapes that are like flavor bombs.

The weather in the area helps the grapes above-ground. The average annual temperature is 13.6 degrees Celsius, a bit warmer than Bordeaux (12.3) and a touch cooler than Tuscany (15.5). The annual sunshine hours add up to 2200—much more than Bordeaux (just 1200) and about as much as Tuscany (2500). But when it comes to rainfall, Brda stands out. All that sunshine is quenched by 1360 millimeters of precipitation a year, while Bordeaux has 950 and Tuscany 920. Brda enjoys an ideal balance of sun, rain, and soil.

Some micro locations within Brda are better than others. As Rusjan explains, "Certain grapes do better at certain locations. Historically, locals would just distinguish between white and red, but in more recent times, they distinguished also between grape varieties and, lastly, biotypes. The best vintners know what area works best with which grapes. Exposure is best facing the south. Then we have altitude as an influence. 100 meters above sea level to 250 meters is best, in terms of an ideal temperature and amount of wind. For Rebula, it should face south, it should be 50-200 meters above sea level, sunny and windy locations are best."

Looking out at the tumble of hills, it's hard to imagine that this was once underwater. That was a while back. In the Mesozoic era, to be precise, around 70 million years ago. This was all the floor of a calcite sea. Earthquakes and tectonic movement pushed the Alps up and the seawater out, eventually relegating it to the Adriatic, which remains nearby. If you slice straight down into the earth at Brda and examine a cross-section of it, you see the soil grouped into horizontal stripes of almost equal width. These were caused when that prehistoric calcite sea wore away at the continental shelf, loosening sediment and causing the rocks around its base to become unstable. The water flow pushed the loose sediment downhill along submarine slopes and deposited it in layers on the ocean floor. It's a bit like someone scraping off bits of wall and pushing these crumbles onto the ground, where they are spread out quite evenly, settling into place, before another layer of wall is shorn off and likewise settles on the floor, atop the previous layer. Fast-forward millions of years and you can see each layer like a horizontal stripe, one stacked upon the next, going back in time. This is the classic flysch formation, with alternating stripes of sandstone and marl, sandstone and marl, over and over. It's not uncommon to find fossils when digging to support new wine terraces, and the area abounds with beautiful crags of the mineral calcite, which looks like white sugar rock candy.

The dry land that was left is very modest in both total area and vineyards. Compare Goriška Brda to the big regions, like Tuscany and Champagne and Bordeaux, and it is *very* boutique: just 1803 hectares of winegrowing area, as compared to 112,000 in Bordeaux, 34,000 in Champagne, and 24,900 in Tuscany. But Brda packs a punch, and Davids have been known to outdo Goliaths. That wine-growing territory may be small in square kilometrage, but it is diverse, with nine distinct sub-regions within Goriška Brda (Neblo, Hruševlje & Hlevnik, Dobrovo, Višnjevik & Krasno, Medana, Vipolže, Šmartno & Kozana, Cerovo, and Kojsko & Hum). 22% of Goriška Brda is dedicated to viticulture, as opposed to 12% in Bordeaux, 1% in Champagne, and 3% in Tuscany.

Rebula itself is always a white grape, but it is divided into four classes: Green, Golden, Petite Berry, and—my favorite—Crazy. If we're getting technical, there are five clones (Rebula SI-30, SI-31, SI-32, SI-33, and SI-34). There are four quality levels of Rebula white: Local, Quality, High Quality, and Sparkling. "With Rebula, there are many biotypes that are quite different, which

Grapes turned to gold by the sun

is unusual among grape varieties," Rusjan explains. "Matija Vertovec wrote one of the best and earliest scientific papers on Rebula back 1844, already identifying six biotypes. Among them, he distinguished Green Rebula, Crazy Rebula, and then with tiny grapes, and so on. These are all still found in Brda. We try to collect them in various vineyards at a national level and save them. In the time of Zvonimir, when he worked with the first sparkling Rebula, in the 70s, he used Rebula with greener grapes. Over the decades, he focused on Yellow or Golden Rebula, which is great for sparkling or still wines."

Hang on, did he say "crazy Rebula?" Is that because it's crazy delicious?

Rusjan smiles and shakes his head. "The term crazy is because it grows crazily quickly. Intensive growth of leaves, and it has very few grapes, and they are all different sizes. Grapes require the most energy when growing, and if there are not many grapes, then the vine and leaves grow much more quickly."

Other wines are grown here, to be sure. And they do well, producing beautiful, award-winning vintages. Rebula makes up the majority, about 20.5% of what is grown. The others of note include Chardonnay (17.4%), Merlot (16.4%), Sauvignonasse/Sauvignon Vert (10.8%), Pinot Grigio (10.4%), Cabernet Sauvignon (6.4%), and Sauvignon Blanc (6%). That 20.5% results in around 170 liters of Rebula produced per resident, with each wine producer making an average 1250 liters per year. But when locals plant new vines, inevitably they are turning to their hometown hero. From 2012-2018, 71% of all new plantings were of Rebula vines. This is the home of Rebula, the place where Rebula grows as perfectly as it can, because this is where it was born. The statistics clearly show that the region embraces its indigenous Rebula, believing in it and dedicated to showing the world the true face of this under-known grape variety, and bringing it to its full potential. I am sure that Miro is watching from above, with happy, proud, smiling eyes.

I was next curious about how Rebula works so well in this particular terroir. Rusjan explained the science of the geology, but what about putting that geology to work? Rebula's international reputation really rose beyond the confines of Yugoslavia in the late 1980s, which is when two Italian gentlemen turned their attention to *Ribolla Gialla*.

Marco Felluga is a long-time friend of Miro's who runs a winery just across the border in Italy. Felluga is a true *gentiluomo*, a gentleman who invited me to his art-filled home to speak about his old friend, Miro, and their mutual love of wine. Now in his 90s, he is dressed immaculately, formally, for our chat, and he glows when speaking about both Rebula, or *Ribolla Gialla* as he calls it, and Miro. His home is just across the border into Italy, in Collio, as is the seat of his winery, Marco Felluga e Russiz Superiore. Felluga exuded sophisticated elegance and it was a real privilege to be invited into his home, knowing what a legend he is among wine specialists.

"At the end of the war, the production was really bad," Felluga begins. "He knew that the viticulture of Brda was having difficulties. There was no market, they didn't know what to do. And I tell you he must've gone thirty times to Ljubljana in order to set up a winery in Brda. And he did it. He made that winery happen. It took a lot of time. But he insisted and persevered until it was done. It saved the community, for they provided the grapes. He told me how often he had to drive to meetings in Ljubljana to make it happen. That was the man. So sensible. He made a new, beautiful winery and, following this, we first got to know each other. He told me what I just told you after the winery had been made. We met each other after. Everyone was talking about Miro, and I went to meet him. I initiated our friendship. Until he won the war, he remained unsatisfied. We reinforced our friendship over the years. He began to set up his own personal vineyard while he was still working at Klet Brda. He was unable to be idle. He helped me, because he really knew all the wine people in the area. He helped me to buy grapes from the best farmers in the region, in Italy and Slovenia. He saw the best opportunity in a regional wine. He resolved the problem for the producers in the area, who didn't have anyone to sell the grapes to locally. He saw the problems and the solutions."

The other gentleman is Attilio Scienza. He stands tall among the wizened professors of wine (which, let's be honest, is just about the best thing anyone could be a professor of). Scienza (whose surname sounds like the Italian for "science"—*nomen est omen*) is a full professor at the University of Milan, in the Department of Agricultural and Food Sciences, and he teaches Viticulture at Master's level at University of Turin. He has been described as Italy's lead researcher into vine genetics, physiology, and agricultural techniques, as evidenced by his authorship of more than 350 publications in journals, monographs, textbooks, and conference proceedings. This includes 23 books in Italian and English. He is a true bon vivant, a larger-than-life character, and an absolute authority.

Scienza recalls, "My experience together with Miro began in 1990, maybe the late 1980s. Miro, Marco Felluga, and I had both a friendship and a consultancy relationship. Friendship

Rebula vines develop root systems that can reach down ten meters or more

and collaboration. When Felluga started producing Rebula at a significant level it became better-known throughout Italy. At the start, Rebula was practically unknown. Chardonnay, Pinot were in fashion. Rebula was marginal. It was always presented in the past as a wine for an osteria. A wine that almost ferments as you drink it. To drink with roasted chestnuts or sliced salami. It didn't have nobility, which foreign varieties did. The goal was to raise its status. Miro essentially invented this approach. His total focus was Rebula. A bit of Merlot maybe, but he really believed in Rebula. But he wanted a noble Rebula, bottled and transported abroad. He studied how to stabilize it, as it didn't travel well. He also invented sparkling Rebula. Now others do it, but he invented it."

Scienza is concerned that Rebula might follow the fate of Prosecco. Now there's nothing wrong with Prosecco, per se, from the perspective of mass consumers. Prosecco is thought of as tasty, cheap "champagne." It's often used as a mixer in cocktails and most people don't think of it as high-end and sophisticated, therefore don't want to pay much per bottle. This is a shame in that Prosecco can be very fine indeed, but the market was long ago set, priced cheap to sell in vast quantities, and so its reputation followed suit. You can make sparkling Rebula using the cheap and swift Charmat or tank method, which is how Prosecco is made. But do that too often and Rebula will be classified as cheap and uncomplicated. Scienza argues that Rebula is far nobler, with a rich historical pedigree and wide array of potential directions a savvy winemaker can take with it. It deserves to be considered among the world's finest high-end wines, with prices to match. This was Miro's dream and Rebula's current reputation is thanks to his determination to raise and maintain Rebula's nobility. "Those who forget history are destined to repeat it," says Scienza. "Miro worked so hard to elevate the status of Rebula from a simple osteria wine to one of high international standing, now I'm worried it is slipping back into cheap status." Due to the fame and increasing demand for Rebula, vintners in Friuli began to plant grapes to make Charmat sparkling wine, a trend that, on the one hand, speaks to Rebula's success, but, on the other, leads Scienza to be concerned that Rebula might slip into a status associated only with cheap sparkling wines, which would be a shame, considering its pedigree and highest-level achievement as a variety. "His story was insufficiently listened to and learned from. It's also important that this is a product of opoka soil. It doesn't do well outside of opoka soil, so it should be made where it is made best." And it's not just opoka soil that's key: Rebula grown uphill on opoka is completely different and far better than Rebula grown in flat-land on rich soil.

There is a counterargument that Prosecco is a household name worldwide, a marketer's dream in terms of product recognition. There will be those who seek out the fancier version of the wine they've heard of. When it comes to champagne, there are those who seek the ten-dollar bottles that are technically champagne and may be tasty (and good for mimosas or Bellinis) but are not going to win any awards. But there is also an audience for the hundred-dollar bottles, the Moëts and Cristals and Veuve-Clicquots. Perhaps that could be the case for Rebula, too, but the focus has been following Miro's lead and keeping it high-end. You can find inexpensive bottles, but the reputation established by Miro is that Rebula is the cream of what white wine can be.

While wine experts know and love it, Rebula remains too little-known to the general wine-consuming public. "Outside of Italy it's hardly known," Scienza continues. "Even in Italy it is slowly becoming better-known, but only in its sparkling form, not as a still wine. Young folks only want to drink sparkling wines. But sparkling is not the destination, the fate of Rebula. The technique Miro used to make his sparkling wine was very different and more complex, the Champagne method with the second fermentation in the bottles, not the quick and inexpensive technique used to make Prosecco. It shouldn't just be an aperitif. There are people prepared to invest in a Prosecco, but that loses the nobility of it. It's a better long-term investment to continue seeing Rebula as a high-end wine. I wrote this book about Rebula in order to lay out the conditions in which Rebula originated and developed. It's a product of two peoples. Until 1918, this was a single people, under Austria, speaking two languages, but a single people and a single territory. After the First World War, the border came, but Rebula is ancient. So before we talk about Rebula as a contemporary issue, we have to see it anthropologically. The origins of Rebula are in opoka soil. It's an easy wine, good for the young, not difficult in terms of profile, structure, aromatics, and with great potential to become a great wine. But the Prosecco Rebula is a pseudo-Rebula, and this should be avoided."

What does Rebula lose when it's grown outside of this area? Denis Rusjan described how two very nearby terroirs, Goriška Brda and the Vipava Valley, less than an hour away, produce different Rebula wines. "If we speak about terroir, we can say that they are different. It is evident in all parameters, statistically and chemically. But we must not say that one is better. That doesn't exist. Terroirs are specifics about an area, not about something being better. The philosophy of terroir is not better or worse, it's just of a certain place. But there are certainly differences in the chemistry of Rebula grapes from these two regions and in terms of taste. But I'm not sure anyone could distinguish better or worse, only different. You can see that Brda is embowered by the Soča River and the Sabotin and Korada hills, and open on other sides. Vipavska Valley is a valley with a forest on one side, Trnovo Forest, and on the other the karst region, pinched between these two natural barriers. It also has a strong Bora wind. All that influences differences in that area and Brda."

What's missing if Rebula is planted in California or Australia? "Everything's missing," Attilio Scienza replies, with a shake of his head. "It becomes an anonymous wine. Rebula isn't aromatic. It gets its personality only when it suffers a bit. Opoka soil makes it suffer. It's a poor soil. The grapes should not grow too quickly, too large or too numerous. We have to be careful of botrytis in other soils. But here it grows just right. It's really a grape that has never spread beyond this region.

My board of experts included Marjan Simčič, whose Rebula Opoka 2016 scored an astonishing 100 points (that's right, out of 100) in a review in *La Gazetta del Vino*. Marjan is the Simčič you're most likely to see on television. He has a lush mane of black hair, clever eyes, and the manner of a 19th-century count, one who recognizes his skill in dealing with the media as an ideal accompaniment to his rightfully feted wines.

It should be noted that there's some confusion among wine fans about the various Simčič vineyards in Goriška Brda. It is a very common surname in this region, and there are three renowned, decorated, and impressive wineries all called Simčič—and none of the families think they are related. I can recommend them all: Marjan Simčič, Edi Simčič and of course the vineyard of our hero, Miro Simčič—Medot. There's even a fourth, Vinska Klet Simčič, which makes a Rebula under the name Simčič and with the names Karol, Igor, and Marjan beneath it. You might think, as I once did, that this was some collaboration between the aforementioned Marjan Simčič and Miro's son, Igor Simčič. Not so. Goriška Brda abounds with Simčičes, several of them called Marjan or Igor, and many involved in making good wine. If you think that's confusing...well, I can only agree with you.

The official inauguration of a monument honoring Zvonimir Simčič. It was attended by the President of the Republic of Slovenia and Slovenian and Italian ministers, mayors, professionals and winemakers. Slovenian and Italian ribbons on the wreath below the monument symbolize its significance on both sides of the border. The photo includes Zvonimir's son, Igor, grandson, Simon, and the mayor, Franc Mužič.

Marjan Simčič emphasizes how important the marriage between variety and landscape is. "Rebula really suits this terroir. On the one hand it's simple, but it has a lot of character. It does not put itself out there. It's not overly aromatic. It does not do as well outside of Goriška Brda and Collio. It requires a lot of sun, higher altitude, and the opoka soil. It needs poor soil with a lot of sunny days and high altitude. It has a root system that can reach down ten meters or more, finding water down deep. If we plant it in richer soil, in a field, for instance, then there are more grapes, but the quality is not good. On the other hand," Marjan continues, "it endures higher summer temperatures well. It ripens late, and we gather the grapes at the same time as Merlot or even Cabernet. These characteristics and even the microclimatic changes suit it. It does well even at 1300 feet in altitude. We see the great results here and, even on the world market, it finds success and praise among the top critics abroad. It is truly the gem of Brda and Collio.

"I have vines that were planted by my father and even my grandfather, some of them eighty years old. I plant all biotypes, but these older ones have excellent grapes, very few of them, but excellent quality. They are particularly tough, they are disease-resistant and rot-resistant, and we can harvest very late."

Franc Mužič is the longest-serving mayor in Slovenia. He has overseen Goriška Brda since 1995 and is still going strong, which makes him the longest-serving mayor in the whole country. Throughout that time, he has been one of the region's greatest promoters, supporting any projects that bring benefit and recognition to his beloved home. I've been told that locals tend to be quite reticent, keeping their opinions to themselves, so I was grateful to find the mayor so open and enthusiastic about my project. He holds Miro in the highest respect and admiration and, like so many people I met from Brda, he is a former employee of Miro's. "There was a time when Rebula was forgotten, sidelined. At that time we, to some extent, forced Rebula forward in order to reestablish it. But Brda was best served pushing our indigenous product. Other varieties found success everywhere, but Rebula is best in certain terroirs, microclimates, altitudes, and Simčič understood this. Young people didn't really understand what the big deal was, but he did. He also saw that Brda had a great advantage in position with the balance of the sea and the high mountains, the Julian Alps. You can see both from Brda. Simčič showed us all what Rebula needed and how to make it world-class. I see lots of potential for

Brda and also Collio regarding Rebula. Rebula will help Brda grow further. We created a House of Rebula at the Dobrovo Castle, of which Zvonimir Simčič is the key protagonist when telling its story." As he made this statement, I could feel the mayor's admiration for Miro, and the House of Rebula is solid evidence of this.

Facing the House of Rebula at Dobrovo Castle, just as I am wrapping up this book, on 4 February 2022, guests from around the world paid homage to Zvonimir Simčič through the unveiling of a monument in his honor. As honorary patron, Borut Pahor, president of the Republic of Slovenia, did the actual unveiling, along with Zvonimir's son, Igor, and grandson, Simon. Because of Zvonimir's professional influence and his role as a pioneer and bridge-builder on both sides of the border, the event was also attended by the Slovenian and Italian Ministers of Agriculture, Forestry and Food, Dr. Jože Podgoršek and Stefano Patuanelli, who held a bilateral meeting at the Castle of Dobrovo prior to the ceremony. Distinguished guests, ambassadors, consuls and mayors from Italy and Slovenia were welcomed in Brda by the Simčič family and the host destination's mayor, Franc Mužič. The event was attended by prominent representatives of the wine profession and outstanding winemakers, including Silvio Jermann, Manlio Collavini, Aleks Simčič, Aleš Kristančič, Marjan Simčič, David Buzzinelli, Paolo Valle di Buttrio, and many others.

6
A BOOK
IS A
JOURNEY

A BOOK IS A JOURNEY

In the process of building the story of Brda wine, Miro published many texts, the most precious of which is a 1987 monograph, now out of print, called *Vino: Med Ljudsko Modrostjo in Sodobno Znanostjo* (*Wine: From Folk Wisdom to Modern Science*). The book is at once a deep and broad introduction to all aspects of wine, from traditions and history to scientific advances and breakthroughs, even covering health, the culture of wine consumption, the role of women in wine, and dinner table etiquette, as well as a treasure trove of Miro's personal warmth and wisdom. When it was published, it was *the* tome of knowledge on winemaking throughout Yugoslavia, a country with a population of some 23 million at the time, and was respected even beyond its borders. It introduced the rules of wine for sommeliers for the first time in this region and thus laid the foundations for all future Slovenian sommeliers.

While he did not invent any specific technological advances, he brought the best of what was available to a region that was far behind. "When they built Klet Brda," Miro's son Igor says, "the Italian side of the equation was somewhat behind the Yugoslav. They carefully studied what we were doing, and I believe were guided and inspired by it. Miro never paid attention to borders. Even though the border was quite serious after the Second World War, he maintained friendships on both sides. Today, when we see internationally successful vintners on the Italian side producing Rebula, they'll still say to me, 'You know why I offer Rebula? Because your father convinced me to.' He looked at Brda-Collio as a single territory, as it always had been before the First World War and was between the wars. There were times when it was labeled as Italy, but people from the area always saw it as one territory, a single terroir. Today, we try to look at this and understand it as a European identity, not divided into countries that are modern inventions."

Miro was not just one to chase dreams but harnessed his dreams to his homeland, the place he felt it was his pride and duty to help move forward and upward. Miro's grandson, Simon, who today runs Miro's family winery, Medot, recalls a story of one of many offers Miro fielded but turned down.

"When he was at the summit of his career, he received an offer from a giant winery in Mendoza, Argentina. The offer included a salary infinitely larger than he could get in Yugoslavia, a house, a car with a chauffeur... He would have complete control over the winery, as oenologist and director, a similar role to what he was doing at Klet Brda, but on a vaster, more lavish scale. He considered it over a long period of time. For his family, it would mean a huge step

Vila Vipolže and the vineyards around it are touched by snow during the winter

Pruning the vines reduces the load of ripening grapes and keeps a golden balance,
resulting in the best quality wine

forward financially. But not in terms of lifestyle. Once he explained that he was headed home from work, and he would always cross the Italian-Slovenian border. Because of the road system around Brda, it was often faster to return to our home via Italy than winding along the roads in Slovenia. When he passed the Yugoslav border office, the guard on duty greeted him, knowing that the director of the winery was on his way home. That might be expected. But then he passed the guard on the Italian side of the border, and he likewise greeted him. That feeling of being respected on both sides of the border was particularly valued in those times, and that respect cannot be bought. He would never have it in Argentina, and so he decided to remain in Brda, where he truly felt at home."

The Italian-Slovenian union was always important to Miro and to Rebula. Claudio Fabbro is an Italian authority on, as he would call it, *ribolla gialla,* and author of a fine book on the subject, *La Ribolla Gialla: Vitigno di Frontiera* (2002). He recalls, "Miro was a friend with whom I shared personal and professional moments of the highest level. When I began as an oenologist, after graduating in Bologna, I began to work for the Collio/Gorizia regional wine cooperative. He told me, 'If you want to improve, for a moment set aside the theory you learned at school and begin to spend time with the people who count, not only in Collio but also in Goriška Brda.' This was the period of 1974-1979, the growers especially around Cormons led in knowledge. But I was encouraged to spend time with the most knowledgeable person around, whether in Italy or elsewhere, and that was Miro. A few months after beginning my work, I found myself at Dobrovo Castle and Miro was there with open arms. He and his team introduced me to the winery and the cellars, to his collaborators. We made a tour of all of Brda together, bright and full of sunshine, covering a lot of kilometers. We ended the day with a good Rebula. I had known little about Rebula."

There was a lengthy list of Italian wine experts who wished to tell their Miro stories. It continued with Pietro Pittaro, who at one time was president of the world society of oenologists and now runs his own vineyard, Vigneti Pittaro, across the border in Friuli. His offering includes a Miro-inspired Ribolla Gialla Spumante, sparkling Rebula made using the classic method.

"I first heard of Miro through rumors that Dobrovo Castle was a place where you could taste wines that were truly avant-garde," Pittaro begins. "I was young then and I arrived by bus at Klet Brda and met Miro. I immediately saw how far ahead he was, despite being, at the time, a young oenologist. This was at a time when cooperative cellars were largely just producing wines labeled 'red' and 'white' that were drinkable and that was it. Talk was only of quantity, not quality. The very idea that you would produce a wine from a cooperative and list the grapes with which it was made was already ahead of the game."

Pittaro and Miro became friends and would meet to exchange ideas over a glass—inevitably—of Rebula. "We would discuss how we could transform the art of wine. We always called it 'the art.' The trick was to harness the goodness that nature provided without losing any of its quality. You know, he was the first in the region to understand and employ the cold technique, which is now used everywhere, to preserve the aroma of the grapes. And then, from that point of departure, what could we do to improve the quality of the end product?"

When I asked what Pittaro saw as Miro's leading characteristic, the simplicity and strength of his answer surprised me. "The answer is straightforward. He saw further than we did." By "we" he meant Italian winemakers contemporary to Miro. This was quite a statement coming from the one-time president of the world oenologist's association. "Miro always had an idea and a half more than the rest of us."

Aleš Kristančič, the head of another star in the Brda wine scene, the Movia vineyard, had similar fond recollections of visits between his father, Mirko, and Miro. Kristančič is one of the great characters of the Slovenian wine world. He's a larger-than-life figure, quite literally. He swoops into a room, moving like a panther, bearing a striking resemblance, in his athleticism, to a famous ancient Hellenistic bronze sculpture, *Boxer of the Quirinale*.

I was immediately taken with his hands. Art historians know that faces and hands were considered the most difficult to paint or sculpt well, so this was where an artist would really show off. And Kristančič has hands that remind me of Michelangelo's *David*. Why? *David* was a statue originally meant to be situated on the façade of Florence's cathedral, therefore seen from far below. For this reason, when we look at *David* from up close, the hands appear disproportionately large. They are designed to appear in proper proportion only when seen from far below. Well, Kristančič has similarly oversized hands that tell their own story—well-used hands, so unlike mine, which do nothing more than type all day.

"He's an artist," said his wife over the phone, apologizing in advance for him regularly appearing late for appointments. "He was even late for his own wedding." But he's certainly worth the wait. An article in *Food & Wine* magazine called him "a genuine and complete showman... intensely focused, passionate and unpredictable...oddly loveable..." I'd agree with all of the above.

There's a local legend that Ernest Hemingway was a fan of Movia wines. He surely drank wines from this region, when he was an ambulance driver during the First World War stationed in this area (and gathering inspiration for his novel, *A Farewell to Arms*). "You know, this is kind of bullshit," Kristančič confides. "During that time, you didn't have a lot of wine. But Movia was always making wine, even during the war. So there is a probability that Hemingway was drinking our wine." Close enough for government work, as the saying goes.

Kristančič was pleased to share his memories of a true legend, Miro. "I remember him as the colossus of Brda," he told me. "He was one of the few people who would come to our house and would leave behind a sort of an aura, even after he left. I was a child at the time, but we would wind up talking about what he'd done, what he'd said, for several days after his visit."

There were two significant roles that Kristančič felt Miro had to embody. "On the one hand, he had to lead our cooperative cellar, Klet Brda, as a promoter. You know, we didn't have a bad wine on the market. We had either correctly made, good wines or great wines. He led the Klet not just as a director, but as a true leader.

"His second role was that he was the first to make classical method sparkling wine out of Rebula. Stepping outside of the norm was only feasible because Klet Brda had a strong, healthy foundation, thanks also to him. His desire to go outside the box was not, at the time, something that you could talk about publicly, but it was a frequent topic of private debate between Miro and my father. They'd speak about this in a whisper."

It might sound odd that such experimentation with wine required covert conversations among old friends and experienced vintners, but in Yugoslavia there was a pressure to maintain the course, not to rock the boat, to fulfill what was expected of you and nothing more. Kristančič went on to say how proud he was that Miro always brought visiting delegations that were coming on official business to Klet Brda also to his family estate ran by his father Mirko, even if they were not members of the cooperative. He would introduce them as an example of a "small, private initiative," despite the fact that they were representing opposite sides, they cooperated and showed recognition and mutual respect among each other. This makes what Miro did, pushing the envelope and blazing new trails, that much more remarkable, once you

At the House of Rebula in Dobrovo Castle, you can taste Rebula wines from the best winemakers in the region, all in one spot

understand the socio-political pressures in which he operated. "I would guess, back then, few people really understood what Miro was all about. What he was aiming for," Kristančič continues. "But if someone has shown you, time and again, that they maybe see farther, know more, than you do, you give them the benefit of the doubt. I even remember my father and uncle saying once, 'With the Medots [the nickname of Miro and his father], you don't always know what they're thinking at any given moment, but time inevitably shows that they're right.'"

All roads in Brda lead to vineyards and each vineyard bears Miro's signature in one way or another. Take the latest project from Silvio Jermann. Jermann was founded in 1881 by Silvio's great-grandfather, Anton. The Jermann family is the perfect trifecta of the region: with Austrian and Slovenian roots, they live just across the border in Italy. The Jermann winery is among the most storied and awarded in the region and that success led to the Tuscan giant, Antinori, buying a majority stake in 2021. Antinori is among the biggest names in world wine, with 26 generations of production and a portfolio of more than twenty estates. Jermann is the latest jewel added to their crown, though Silvio Jermann will continue to be the "soul" of the vineyard. Silvio is constantly smiling with a Puckish, knowing glow in his eye.

"Whenever my father would drive me through Brda to go to Klet Brda," Jermann recalls, "he would mention this famous oenologist. When I was younger, I could never figure out how to pronounce his name! For a young Italian boy, Zvonimir is not easy to say. The parallel my father would draw was that Zvonimir was to Slovenia what Mario Schiopetto was to Italy."

I'll admit that I had to look up Mario Schiopetto, but I quickly learned that he is considered the pioneer of modern white wine in Friuli. He began his career as a truck driver, but always loved wine and learned as much as he could during travels in Germany and France. He created the first Tocai in Italy (though it is no longer called that) and introduced new technologies that are in ubiquitous use today. Though a bit younger than Miro, I could immediately see why Jermann's father would compare the two revolutionary, forward-thinking vintners, one in northeastern Italy, the other in Yugoslavia.

"Zvonimir immediately conferred a sense of capability, knowledge, and nobility of bearing. My father was really fascinated by him. Particularly his technical brilliance. My father was a great winemaker but never studied oenology formally, so he was fascinated by Zvonimir's knowledge. Zvonimir managed to create a new wine, a modern wine. He also sorted out not only the quality but the commercial viability, and we all know that these two don't always co-exist in harmony. He was good at this even during difficult times. I appreciate his focus on Rebula, because Rebula is the image of Brda."

And what did Jermann do as his first project after the sale of Jermann to Antinori? He leads me outside onto the terrace and points to the crest of a hill in the near distance. "This is my latest project," he says. "I planted a new vineyard on the best possible location and orientation. And I planted it exclusively with Rebula, of course!"

The first president of Slovenia, Milan Kučan, also shared some memories of Miro—who he refers to as "Zvonko." He first encountered Rebula when he bought a bottle to open on the day of his daughter's birth, a bottle he still keeps as a souvenir, in fact. At that point, this being long before he was president and Slovenia was an independent nation, he had never been to Brda and decided to pay a visit to see the land that had produced so elegant a wine.

He remembers his first visit, arriving at the crest of a hill overlooking the villages of Brda and seeing a giant monument shaped like a wine glass with "Vino di Brda" written across it. This was clearly the right place. He met Miro during that first visit, and they had many further meetings, having hit it off straight away.

"Brda today bears Zvonko's imprint," he said in an interview that he conducted exclusively for this book. "He was a man ahead of his time. He knew France, he knew Italy, and what he found abroad he wished to establish in his hometown. He saw the identity of Brda in the grapes and wanted them to be made into wine at the spot where they grew, not sold abroad and mixed with other grapes. It was his idea to establish a collective winery, Klet Brda, and allow the people of Brda to produce their own wine."

"At the time that Zvonko wanted to establish Klet Brda, the wine of Brda was under-appreciated," Kučan continues. "Other areas of Slovenia, like Styria, were more associated with wine. In fact, the thought at the time was that anyone wanting to learn about wine had to go to Styria to do so." In Miro, there was someone who had learned abroad, in Italy, and that trumped even the best of Slovenian cellars in Styria.

Miro's focus on a local wine was also compelling. "Anytime I went to visit Zvonko," Kučan recalls, "he would offer me a glass of Rebula. It was the same when I visited the cellar of Mirko Movia. A glass of sparkling wine but only Rebula."

Their friendship continued. Even when Kučan was president, he found time to attend Miro's 75th birthday party. "When I looked around the room at the guests assembled for the part," he says, "I thought, wow, this is a man who is equally respected in Italy as he is at home. And this wasn't simply a matter of tipping your hat at someone who lives on your border, but there was true appreciation for him as someone whose knowledge was so deep that he could offer wisdom to Italian vintners, as well."

Kučan has a special phrase that he uses to complement those who truly impress him with their will and innovation, going against the grain and succeeding. "He kicks a blackberry bush barefoot," Kučan says of Miro. The path may be painful but true innovators do what others choose not to, or don't think to.

7

THE JOURNEY TO THE CELLAR

THE JOURNEY TO THE CELLAR

Miro's book was written when Klet Brda was well-established and thriving. By this time, I'd heard so much about the largest winery in the country that I figured it was now time to visit the bastion which Miro saw built and from which he led the Yugoslavian wine crusade, with Rebula leading the charge. As with any of my in-person visits, my inner historian obliges me to dip into the rich history of the region, and slowly make my way up in time to the present.

In the village of Dobrovo, as the road curves tightly between acres of neatly planted vines, a striking architectural form suddenly emerges. Like a colossus hunkered down close to the hillside, the concrete forms of Klet Brda might be mistaken for a fortress, or perhaps the entrance to a Yugoslav space agency. Its most prominent feature is a cylindrical concrete tower that looks like it might take off at any moment. As an art historian with a doctorate in Slovenia's greatest architect, I'm loving it. I find beauty in brutalist concrete structures and monuments, of which there are many across the former Yugoslavia. That this happens to be a monument to wonderful wine makes it only better.

In true socialist fashion, Klet Brda works as a coop. Four-hundred and eighty families, most of which have worked with the winery since its earliest years, provide grapes and labor. The wines are exported to twenty-six countries as of writing, and they represent the highest-quality and most recognizable wine label in Slovenia. They are also by far the biggest in the country (and, needless to say, in tiny Goriška Brda), producing over four million bottles per year.

When Klet Brda opened its doors in 1957 it was the first new winery in the region that had once only seen wine made in the premises of the seventeen castles in the area, which were all owned by foreign nobles. It was started as a cooperative and remains so, owned exclusively by a collective of local wine growers. It is the pinnacle of the area's rich history of wine.

If we travel back in time as far as wine traces may be found, we hit the date of 300 BC. That's the carbon dating result on grape pips found by archaeologists in the village of Golo Brdo. The agricultural cultivation of wine dates to circa 100 AD, when the Romans, who occupied the region, employed a viticulture method of growing vines on fruit trees, rather than the modern trellises (a method that was favored until the very end of the 19th century). Wine was stored and transported in terracotta amphoras, vessels with a conical bottom that would seem impractical (surely they would fall over), but in fact they were "seated" in sand or in a wooden lattice with hay, tied together, to travel with minimal clunking and breakage. Enough wine was produced in this area that there was an amphora manufacture found by archaeologists in an ancient home called Villa Rustica in today's village of Neblo.

The tradition of wine in the region continued unabated into the period of recorded history. There are mentions of it as planted as far away as Treviso, south to Koper on the Istrian peninsula, and in parts of Venice. In the Middle Ages, it was referred to as *vinum navigatum*. In 1336, Rebula is first mentioned in a surviving document in Brda, named in a contract for the purchase of property in the village of Višnjevik. The survival of the contract makes for charmingly specific reading. It was signed on 27 May 1336 and relates that Henry from Rittersberg bought a vineyard here for the price of 8 marks, and that the vineyard produced 6 "buckets" of Rebula annually. (I tried, without success, to figure out a conversion rate for 8 marks and 6 "buckets" in the 14th century to today's equivalents—we professors have our limitations). Wine was preferred white and sweet, of a type and taste that is likely closest to today's "sweet filtered" wines. Rebula is well-suited to producing the favorite taste of wine's early history, though its versatility means that it has also been adapted to the 20th-century appreciation for dry wines.

Viticulture in this part of the world was preserved and cultivated at the estates surrounding monasteries. In the Brda region, the most important was Rosazzo Abbey (Abbazia di Rosazzo), who produced a popular Rebula that was sold to the German market, providing the primary income source for the abbey. Another monastic record comes from the monastery of San Secondo in Venice. There, a nun called Florienita is recorded as having left her son, who lived in Piran, on the Adriatic coast of what is now Slovenia, rights to a vineyard for the oddly precise period of exactly 39 years, on one condition: that they use the land to provide at least 150 liters of "good quality Rebula" for the monastery. Archives in Piran include numerous instances of contracts requiring the provision of Rebula as a form of payment of debt. It seems to have been deemed a category higher than any other wine available, as it is the only wine mentioned by specific name, not simply called "wine."

A specific type of feudalism reigned in this region until the 20th century, an unbelievably long time, near two centuries longer than the feudal system in most of Europe. This is referred to as *colonato* or "colonate," though if you Google "colonate feudalism," as I did (I may be a professor, but this term was new to me), you get exactly zero hits in English. This means that it wants explaining, and understanding it helps to comprehend how Brda remained unable to pull itself onto its feet economically...until the benevolent intervention of Miro and Klet Brda gave it a cash crop—grapes made into wine—that found a significant market all year round (as opposed to their seasonal bounty of cherries and plums.

The *colonato* system was a sort of halfway step between the slave system that ran the Roman Empire (with landowners owning their human workforce) and the feudal system that we come to associate with medieval Europe. In traditional feudalism, nobles oversaw serfs who worked their land. Serfs were indentured servants whose lives were not dissimilar to those of slaves. They were not technically owned by the lord, but they leased land and a home from him in exchange for giving him a percentage of the crops they farmed. The lord ostensibly defended them and was their judge and ruler. Serfs had little chance of leaving or improving their lot, and there was frequent abuse of power on the part of the lord. This almost precisely defines the *colonato* system, a slight variation in which the serfs (called, rather optimistically, "colonists") were free but were not logistically able to leave the land they leased from the lord (though they were legally, theoretically permitted to leave). They cultivated the land in exchange for a "canon," an annual rent that they could pay either in money or in crops. This developed particularly around the Mediterranean, filling in the gap left when the Roman Empire disintegrated and rose alongside the first Christian emperors (there is a parallel with *stratiotas* in the Byzantine Empire).

The first "colonists" were former slaves who became freemen and chose to remain where they were, or shift to the land of a neighboring lord, and continue the sort of work they'd done (or their ancestors had) as slaves, though now free in name if not exactly in practice. A key distinction that made being a colonist preferable to being a serf is that colonists were not judicially subject to their lord. They could marry only with the lord's permission (in most cases serfs could not) and they could acquire goods (sometimes serfs could not)—though if the colonist wanted to sell goods on, they had to get consent of the lord, since logic suggested that acquisition of goods would positively affect agricultural returns on the land. If the lord sold the land on which a colonist lived, then the colonist and their responsibilities were transferred to the new owner. Like serfs, once someone agreed to be a colonist, their descendants were obliged to likewise be colonists on that land until the lord or a court authorized their leaving.

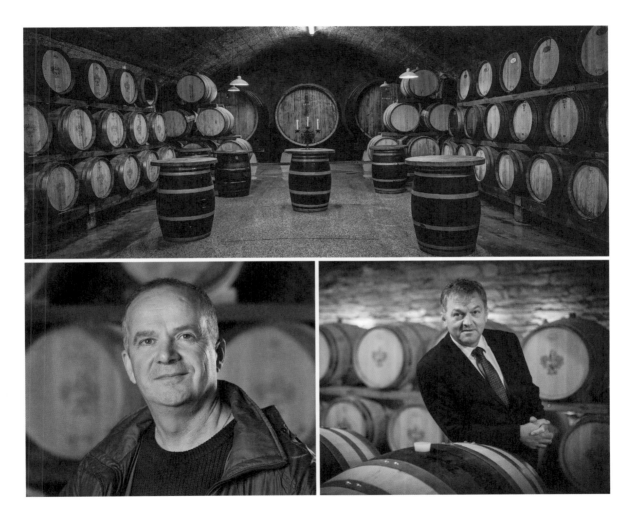

Klet Brda, where Darinko Ribolica is the oenologist and Silvan Peršolja is the director

The de Baguer cellar at Dobrovo Castle, next to the Klet Brda, serves as a new addition, featuring only their top wines

Count de Baguer was one such lord, albeit a benevolent one. If Miro was the man who brought the world's top wine-making innovations to the region in the 20th century, his 19th century counterpart was Count Silverji de Baguer.

De Baguer was born on 2 December 1838 in Odessa, where his father, Jaime, was the Spanish consul. In June 1872 he married Cecilia de Catterini-Erzberg, the sole child of an aristocratic family from Goriška Brda. (The details of his love for the servant girl, and where that fits into his marriage to Cecilia, have been lost to history, or rather the official history only mentions Cecilia as de Baguer's wife, and does not weigh in on whom he loved). Through Cecilia, he inherited Dobrovo Castle. The castle was first built in the 13th century, but the original, medieval fortress is no longer visible. On its ruins a 17th century villa was built, in the Neo-Renaissance style, and that is what we see today. The first owners of the renovated villa were the Counts of Colloredo, followed by the Marquis of Montecuccoli. From the end of the 18th century, the Catterini-Erzberg family lived there, until it passed, through marriage to de Baguer. The renovated villa had a wine cellar that was maintained by the Counts of Colloredo, who kept their wine in giant barrels. But it was de Baguer who transformed this from a simple storage cellar into a proper center for wine cultivation and archiving.

By profession, de Baguer was a diplomat, working for many years as the Spanish ambassador to the Holy See in the Vatican. He introduced Brda wines to the papal cellars. He is credited with bringing wine cultivation to the region, recognizing its potential as a terroir (long before anyone thought in terms of terroir). He planted the first vines in 1880, and his vineyards expanded to cover 315 hectares, producing 12,000 hectoliters of wines per year. Grapes were grown and wine was made in the region before his arrival, of course, but he helped to develop it in a more organized way, at a grander scale, and implemented leading technologies and scientific advances of the time. During his lifetime, sweet wines were preferred in this area, and he helped develop a taste and fashion for dry wines aged in glass bottles. He was also an early oenophile who kept an extensive archive of wines, and notes on cultivation and what he had tasted. He was an enthusiast for the local Rebula variety, and in this way was a predecessor of Miro's crusade.

De Baguer made a science of it before it was a science: how many vines were planted, how much the yield was, what the wine was like, and so on. He began to proactively plant vineyards and archive his collection of wines in 1880, dividing them into nine categories. From 1909 he started to build cellars beneath Dobrovo Castle, his main residence. He installed three concrete cisterns, which he lined with glass. This was the highest level of wine-making technology at the time, an invention from scientists in Klosterneuburg, Austria, which was the center for wine knowledge and experimentation for the Austro-Hungarian Empire.

Ivan Peršolja, president of the Slovenian Sommelier's Association, concurs, saying "The standard of quality was the key to expanding the market and branding Brda as a world center for wine. Our wine was valued in the Austro-Hungarian Empire, thanks to Count de Baguer, who did great things. Each period finds a person who leads and leave a legacy, and we build from it. Each period takes a step or two forward, and this is important when we look back into history. The development of Klet Brda was the key moment for Brda and for wine in Slovenia. Before then everyone did their best without training and without broader experience beyond their family traditions."

Count de Baguer died on 27 April 1927, leaving his estate to his firstborn daughter, Elvira.

De Baguer was such an influential figure, the driving force in shifting Goriška Brda from a humble place where wine was made primarily for local consumption into a place associated with good wine, that the prestige range of wines produced by Klet Brda are sold under the label Bagueri, as a nod to the most direct predecessor as godfather of viticulture in the region. With this tradition in mind, in 2019 Klet Brda reopened the historic de Baguer cellar at Dobrovo Castle, which is now home to the Bagueri and A+ lines produced by Klet Brda. These are aged in French and Italian barriques and egg-shaped wooden barrels, as well as *pupitres*, A-frame wooden racks for riddling sparkling wines produced according to the classic method.

Not only did he introduce modern technology, circa 1894, to the millennia-old viticulture traditions and but, like Miro, he also carefully wrote out the wine practices in the area, which proved a great boon to historians. The only major advance in this era came after the 1870 infestation of grape louse (phylloxera), which nearly obliterated all of the vineyards in the area. To counteract this, locals took to grafting resistant rootstock onto their vines, which proved successful in combating the infestation. De Baguer also oversaw a new experiment in 1881—planting vineyards without the use of fruit trees to support them, a foretaste of the modern trellis system.

The *colonato* system was surprisingly long-lived. As late as 1922, there were still thirty-eight "colonists" who, according to record, established the first cooperative in Brda, buying 230 hectares of land from their landlord. It was the beginning of the end of the *colonato* system here.

This was a system rigged by nobility to guarantee a sufficient agricultural workforce even with slavery dissolved. That something along these lines was in place until the second half of the 20th century helps explain why the residents of Goriška Brda had trouble pulling themselves forward into modernity and economic stability. For them, a foreign noble presence lasted until the end of Austro-Hungarian/Habsburg rule, and the sudden, rather arbitrary division of their homeland into an Italian and a Slovenian side, after the First World War. The arrival of socialism would have been welcomed as a step forward. The authority was now the State and socialism in Yugoslavia was the most lenient and citizen-friendly of all the socialist experiments, nowhere more so than in Slovenia. But Goriška Brda was still without industry and economic means beyond those desirable cherries. The answer to the business and economics question came in 1957 with the establishment of Klet Brda—the Brda wine cellar. This was preceded two years earlier by the formation of a more extensive wine-making cooperative in Brda, which began to build a new wine cellar in Dobrovo. These 400 wine-growing families had, just a generation before, been mostly "colonists," so this marked a big step toward independence and financial stability. That was the point of departure for Miro Simčič to lobby with the powers that be, in Ljubljana and Belgrade, to expand this into Yugoslavia's lead winery. This project was initially slated for construction in the nearest city, Nova Gorica, but Miro's intervention led the decision for it to be built in the Dobrovo village of Goriška Brda.

Miro brought Yugoslavia's biggest wine project to his home, and in doing so created the main industry for the region from that point forward.

Overseeing Klet Brda, Miro helped plan the elaborate winery construction, with all the modern amenities. He guided its business and production for decades. He was responsible for the focus on hyper-local Rebula and the introduction, for the first time anywhere, of the first sparkling Rebula made with the Charmat method, production of which began in 1962. The largest yield to date came in 1979, ringing in at 150 million kilograms. Klet Brda wines were treasured in Yugoslavia as the highest-end beverage, but also enjoyed abroad, with the first export to the US in 1984. Demand was such that, by 1991, the Klet Brda policy focused on export. This coincided with Slovenia's independence from Yugoslavia. That year Slovenia became its own sovereign nation and trade possibilities opened up that previously would have required extensive bureaucratic acrobatics. In 2002, more than a million bottles were sold worldwide. In 2017, Klet Brda was producing some 4 million bottles a year.

Klet Brda has been recently awarded the prestigious Green Key for long-term sustainable production. Their combination of expansion, eco-sustainability, and the highest quality means that the legacy begun by Miro has continued in the right hands.

* * * * *

I forgot about the ricochet effect. My trousers would suffer for it, but it was a sacrifice worth making. But I'm losing the through-line already, even before we get to my expectorate inadequacies. This is possibly because my day in March 2021 was possibly the best day of the last year. Or perhaps because I tasted a dozen wonderful wines that day. Or for these reasons combined.

I began researching and writing this book in 2019 and finished in in 2022. There was a year in between that was less-than-ideal for the inhabitants of Planet Earth. The pandemic meant that my March 2021 visit to Goriška Brda, to tour Klet Brda and taste their offerings and to tour the Medot Winery and taste theirs, as well, was my first outing in nearly a year. Heck, it was practically the first time I put on trousers in nearly a year, after having lounged my way through 2020 in pajama pants. This led me to the conclusion that trousers are both celebratory and rather restrictive. Why didn't we all just use 2020 to shift to the concept of "business from the waist up, sleepy time from the waist down?" So today I spat upon trousers. Sounds like a metaphor, right? If only...

So my plan was to visit as many wineries in Goriška Brda that produce Rebula as I could, in as short a time as possible, while following the safety constraints that 2021 required. It would be a whirlwind tour, but that's part of the fun. Nims Purja wasn't the first human to climb all fourteen 8000-meter-tall mountains on Planet Earth. That was Reinhold Messner. But Messner took sixteen years while Purja did it in just seven months. Most tourists would give themselves a good week to taste their way through the delights of Goriška Brda wineries. But I am not most tourists. What if I could sip them all in, say, a single day?

It would turn out to require more visits to do the region justice (fair enough). There was just so much to see, do, hear, taste, and learn that I wound up spending a full day soaking in the atmosphere of Miro's Rebula fortress.

My day began at Klet Brda, where I was joined by my friend Eldina—she was the first to invite me to the Masterclass back when I wrote about it for the Slovenian edition of *Playboy*. We sat in the office of Silvan Peršolja. While there were a number of directors of Klet Brda between Miro, its founder, and Silvan, they are the two great flagbearers of the winery, with Silvan the inheritor of Miro's torch.

I wanted to learn the history of Klet Brda from Miro onward, and Silvan has served as director since 1998. He is tall and gregarious, welcoming. He smiles through his eyes. Inside his office, my eyes were immediately drawn to an enormous painting of a matronly Goriška Brda grandmother with a full basket of sour cherries on her lap and a look of disapproval on her face. Perhaps this is a good reminder that Klet Brda is the pride, and primary economic stimulus, of the area and so Silvan and his team must work hard not to disappoint a *nonna* such as this one?

My goal was to understand the story of Klet Brda, which is necessarily also the story of Miro, who passed the torch of leadership on to Silvan. I spoke to many people about all aspects of the story, but here I sat, in the office of the inheritor of Zvonimir's professional legacy, as director of Klet Brda. There is something magical about being in the space once occupied by someone about whom you're researching and writing. When I wrote a biography of the Renaissance artist and the godfather of art history, Giorgio Vasari, I knew that I needed to be in his home in Arezzo and inside the corridors of the Uffizi, which he designed, to "vibe" with my subject. So it was that I felt an atmospheric closeness to Miro by visiting the offices he once ruled over and the winery he built.

"If we look at the arc of Zvonimir's career," Silvan began, "from his start studying viticulture in Conegliano, he was technically ahead of the game. He was trained, he knew modern winemaking. This training made him respected in Yugoslavia and he was able to influence a shift in plans. Instead of making the Klet as one big conglomerate in Nova Gorica, they went with his suggestion and planned build one in Goriška Brda and one in Vipava. This showed his recognition of the importance of terroir." He was politically astute in that he didn't pick sides and was seen as somehow above the machinations of Yugoslav politics, the need to be an overt member of the Socialist Party in order to advance. He was seen as unique in the country, with his training and the international connections with Italy. This gave him far greater license than one would think at the time, when the only directors of major Yugoslav firms were diehard socialists.

"The other key," Silvan continues, "was Zvonimir's absolute determination that each terroir should be known by its indigenous variety. And for Brda it was Rebula, Rebula, Rebula." There was a time when the world market was hyper-focused on Merlot, and so the farmer's cooperative argued that they should meet the demand and plant mostly Merlot. Zvonimir wasn't an absolutist—he planted Merlot, but he was always adamant that 'Rebula would be the fille rouge. We'll be known for Rebula, or we won't be known.'"

I was curious if there was a definitive answer to the debate about which I'd read, as to whether Rebula might actually hail from elsewhere around the Mediterranean. For instance, there's a Greek variety called Robola found exclusively on Ionian islands of Kefalonia, Greece. Since Brda falls roughly along the overland spice trade route that linked the Byzantine Empire to the Venetian Empire, some wondered whether Robola was brought from what is now Greece and planted in this part of the world, making it an ancient settler but not truly indigenous. To answer this question, a genetic study was undertaken in 2012, using genotyping to examine the genetic "fingerprints" of Ribolla Gialla from the Friuli-Venezia Giulia region, Rebula from Brda and Robola from the Ionian islands of Greece. The resulting Simple Sequence Repeats (SSR) in the genotypes show that Ribolla Gialla and Rebula are identical in all 35 SSR markers. Robola differs to some degree, though it is likely closely connected to Ribolla Gialla/Rebula. This confirmed that the Italian and Slovenian grapes are exactly the same, with merely the terminology differing. The possibility remains that several thousand years ago the first vines were Robola brought by traders from Greece and planted in Brda/Collio. Whatever the case, Brda/Collio is where Rebula was established, where it thrives, where its reputation as the most valued wine from this part of the world from the Middle Ages through the Habsburg Empire was solidified, and where it was elevated, in more recent years, to a place among the world's best whites.

"Rebula is his greatest legacy," Silvan continues. "It was a historical wine. But this was an era of international varieties. Rebula was seen as a wine for workers, for spritzers, for home use. With his stubbornness he stuck with Rebula." Silvan pauses to think. "He introduced some

The undulating Brda/Collio region, with its distinctive vineyards on terraces, with Klet Brda and Dobrovo Castle in the background

advances, like Golden Rebula and the sparkling variety. He brought the quality to the level when a prestigious hotel, Esplanade in Zagreb, was ordering enormous quantities. In the 80s, the city of Zagreb alone was ordering a million bottles a year. That was colossal. Famous artists, like the actor, Rade Šerbedžija, are fans of Golden Rebula. Last year he visited the winery and asked to taste it. Every field is known for someone. Every place is known for something. For Brda, that someone is Miro and that something is Rebula."

In the 70s, Klet Brda was expanded from its original form (little more than the distinctive concrete cylinder of the main processing building), and new technology was integrated. It was a time when Yugoslavia could not produce enough wine to meet the demand (which was primarily for internal consumption, not for export), and so the focus was on quantity.

"At the end of the 70s," Silvan continues, "when I was a student and we went for work experience at Klet Brda, we came to realize that, after the Second World War, Brda was cut in half, between Italy and Slovenia. There was no work, the farmer's cooperative couldn't provide infrastructure for its constituents to live comfortably off the land. Many moved away. Then the idea arrived to make a winery. This seemed ideal for the area, with its traditions of growing fruit and making wine at a modest level. But when the winery was conceived, it was really a megalomaniacal project. The plan was to produce 850,000 liters of wine a year at the start and to develop it to the point where it would produce 4 million liters a year. A great, visionary project. Who was behind this? Miro was one of them and the key player. He offered his knowledge to the project, his schooling in winemaking at the best-known oenological school. Then, because of his connections with the Partisans (the leading political party), he had access to decision-makers. He knew how to present his ideas and who to present them to so that they moved forward through the system and his ideas reached decision-makers in a favorable way. He had a business sense that often is lacking. And he did not compare himself to other Yugoslav projects, as was the norm at the time, but looked internationally. He did not see obstacles as catastrophes but as something that you have to work around and overcome. Things like a local protest against building such a giant winery—this was not something you encountered and then gave up, but something to figure out how to solve. That spirit flourished at the winery and among those who worked for him. He would always ask us, 'What do you think? What would you do here?' He was like a strict teacher, but he empowered us."

Most wine was sold by the liter at the time. You bring your own bottle or jug to the winery and pay for what you pour. This was the cheaper approach. The fancier option was to buy the wine already dosed into labeled bottles—how most of us buy wine today. Despite the urgency for quantity, Zvonimir assured that the quality never dropped. Wine by the liter, which is normally of lesser quality than more expensive bottled wine, was for decades thought to be *better* than its bottled sibling in Yugoslavia. Product quality was king and it was important to Miro that he had the best technology available, in order to make wine that was on par with the best international wineries. He liked to say, "If you're going to race, and all your competitors have cars with 3000 horsepower, you can't arrive with a car with just 1000."

During this time the brand was expanded thanks to the Croatian actor, Rade Šerbedžija (he is still a Hollywood regular), promoting Klet Brda, but specifically "Moja Rebula." At the time, Rebula wasn't as well-known across the border in Collio. The major Italian producers today were in part inspired by Zvonimir to focus on their indigenous vine, a fact that one of the best, Marco Felluga, readily confirms: [Miro] had a Rebula white wine, and he produced it before we Italians did. Then we began to plant it more ourselves. It sold well and was good quality. The market was really open to it. We producers knew it would sell, so we produced it with tranquility. It has typical characteristics of the region."

Before the First World War, Rebula was the most planted vine in both Collio and Brda, but after World War Two fashion shifted to the big international grapes, like Sauvignon, Chardonnay, and Merlot. Miro's laser focus on Rebula was emotional, Silvan explains. "The numbers at the time didn't show a market for it. It was more the idea that you must become known for something special. For us it wasn't going to be Merlot, it wasn't going to be Pinot Grigio." These were the two most a la mode grapes at the time, but they were grapes from elsewhere, from everywhere. This determination that Rebula was the way Klet Brda, and through it Goriška Brda, would become known was not the least bit self-evident outside of Miro's mind and circle. "If you'd asked ten vintners at the time about Rebula," Silvan jokes, "they would've laughed and said, 'What are you talking about, Rebula?' Who's interested in that? It's Sauvignon and Pinot Grigio that people want."

Claudio Fabbro has similar recollections. "In Collio, starting in 1968, we had developed a wine called Collio Bianco, made up of Rebula 50% and the rest Tocai and Malvazia. So, we were not talking about pure Rebula. It was a neutral, fresh, acidic, easy-drinking, and Rebula gave to the other varieties what they lacked alone. Rebula has an exuberance. The message from Miro was that we should begin to shift programs and focus on Rebula, but he was aware that bureaucracy in Italy is tremendous. It takes twenty years to make a single change. He put out two ideas: Ribolla Gialla, Yellow Rebula, and also a brut made of Rebula. There was also a green Rebula, the yellow and the green. The green variety was considered less sophisticated than the yellow. We ended that day with a great tasting of Brda specialties, and there is no lack of them. Not only fruit and wine, but specialties based on pig, like prosciutto and suckling pig, cheeses. And a good Rebula."

Fabbro continues. "Miro was a unique person. He had studied in Italy, spoke perfect Italian, even with a Friulan dialect. He was calm but with a very, very strong character. In our terroir of Collio we had planted mostly French grape varieties (Pinot Noir, Pinot Gris). These beautiful terraces of wine, built on opoka soil and fanned by the Bora wind, is ideal for white wine of the highest quality. These foreign varieties, of course, will make fine wines. But to truly satisfy, do not forget your own history. This was Rebula. Do not forget it, he said, even when clients want Pinot Grigio, Pinot Noir. These days, everyone wants Prosecco. I didn't know anyone who made Prosecco. Now very few want sweet wines. We were at a turning point. The Azienda where I worked needed to move forward. It could not live off of memories. So we turned to Rebula for the future, while still catering to the needs and demands of the present market. We had to look ahead, maybe 15, maybe 20 years. Back then, time stretched out. These days everything is in a hurry. Miro said, 'Move forward, but never forget your roots.' I said, 'Miro, these days everyone wants to buy Pinot Grigio.' He replied, 'Okay, we'll also give them a bit of good Pinot Grigio.' He was more for cleaner, simpler wines. Not extreme ones. There was an era of experimentation, and this territory was an enclave of Slavic wine makers, like Joško Gravner. But Miro was in favor of purity. His message was 'Look ahead, far ahead. But don't forget your roots. The great wines can grow only after a lifetime of 15, 20 years. If a vine grows for 2 years, it will give you a light wine. Place down your roots, then give them time to grow into great wines.' His idea was to plant Rebula now and not to expect great things of it for a generation. We have this problem with Prosecco. It's planted and then there's too much of a hurry for it to produce good wine. You can't have a man of 20 produce ten great children by the age of 30. It's too rushed, too much too soon. We should use classical methods to make great wines."

Miro stuck by his principles and was never cowed by politicians or other directors. There was importance given to status symbols in a socialist system in which, theoretically at least, everyone was equal. That's one of the key differences between Socialism and Communism, which are often used as interchangeable terms in the Anglophone world (before I moved to Slovenia, I didn't really know there was a difference). Yugoslav socialism was such that all employment and care for citizens was handled by the State, but there were discrepancies in income, depending on one's level within a State-run enterprise. Managers made more than line workers and less than directors. To become a director meant that you had to be an enthusiastic and loyal member of the Socialist Party, but membership was optional. Miro is one of the few exceptions, as a director thanks to the respect he garnered and the expertise he developed, not due to political favors or machinations.

Many who knew Miro described him as having an aristocratic bearing and the authority of a benevolent monarch. He also intentionally played the part as a tactic. Throughout Yugoslavia, the mark of excellence was Germany—their economy, their products, their cars. So, Miro used a black Audi. But he wouldn't drive it himself. Instead, he had a chauffeur. This was how the biggest of the bigshot Yugoslav directors and politicians would roll. It was Miro's equivalent of racing with a V12 engine car when he went to meetings in Ljubljana or even Belgrade, the Yugoslav capital. "He wouldn't look like a small potato director from the countryside, but like the Boss," Silvan smiles. "With a chauffeur. And the chauffeur's surname was Fikfak."

Did I hear that name correctly? I hadn't even started tasting wines, but the name sounded so cartoonish that I thought I might have. It was correct. Miro's chauffeur was named Veri Fikfak. Let the record show that this name sounds very funny even to Slovenes. But what is important is that Miro had a chauffeur. This was a very rare occurrence in Yugoslavia, even among directors of major factories or firms.

It was clear that Miro knew how to roll. When he would attend meetings of various Yugoslav directors, there was no way he could be mistaken for a country cousin, even if the company he ran was as much on the periphery as one could get. He bore himself like a nobleman, with calm, understated confidence and authority, the confidence and authority of someone who truly possesses it, not someone who feels the need to overtly demonstrate it because they are uncertain inside.

It's important to understand the nature of the time in which Klet Brda thrived. While it sounds old-fashioned today, it was key then for Zvonimir to present himself as a gentleman in the sense that other directors of Yugoslav state firms and politicos would understand. Zvonimir was a gentleman, but he was obliged to play a caricatured version of the role. Otherwise, when he would attend meetings in Ljubljana or even Belgrade, he risked being dismissed as a bumpkin living, it must be recalled, in one of the poorest regions in Yugoslavia. As Simon Simčič says, "When he stepped in as director, Brda was among the poorest regions in Slovenia. To help you understand, I have memories of the Slovenian version of Monopoly, the first property you land on, the cheapest...that was Brda. When the winery was built in Brda, and not in Nova Gorica, that was a big early victory for Nonno (Grandfather). It essentially rescued Brda from poverty and provided work for scores of residents."

Vili Mišigoj was one of them. "This was a man for Brda. He meant a new era for Brda. I remember from the early days that we, in Brda, knew that Miro was an expert, in love with winemaking and wine, and that he had studied in Italy. And we hoped that he would return to Brda and stay and help us start an era of winemaking here. It was so poor here, but there was a tradition of Counts here who did not support education and independence, but whose interest was in just keeping the territory for themselves and keeping the locals as workers. The Second World War changed everything about this and life in Brda. And Engineer Simčič saw this opportunity to improve things and drove us in the right direction.

"Prior to working in Brda, he spent time at work in Šempeter pri Gorici. And all he talked about was coming back to Brda. It was around 1950 that he came to Brda to see how the small wineries here functioned after the nationalization of private property. The Count's property was seized by the Yugoslav government and so he came to inspect the state of the vineyard and cellars formerly owned by the Count and the local farmer's cooperative. They were without leadership or expertise or training. Mister Simčič and a few others associated with our national agricultural institutes came to inspect and to help. In Brda we did not speak much about Rebula grapes, or other varieties. We just said, 'We have good wine.' Rebula was something special, but it was largely forgotten. It did not have a lead role. That role was something that Simčič gave it. Before Simčič arrived, the only proper winery was the Count's, otherwise families had their own, small-scale winemaking but just within the family and a bit beyond.

Then Klet Brda began, and Engineer Simčič had this preoccupation, this desire for that winery to rescue Brda as a whole. Engineer Simčič and Professor Veselič from University of Ljubljana brought technique and technology to Brda for the first time. He decided that Rebula would become synonymous with Brda. It was not associated with the neighboring wine region of the Vipava Valley or anywhere else at the time. Vipava Valley had the same grapes, but they called them Grganja. When the time came for Klet Brda to begin producing, Engineer Simčič became the lead organizer and oenologist, he focused on Rebula. 'Rebula, yes, but it must be from Brda' was a slogan that he chose and promoted. That annoyed quite a few people. When it came to selling wine, he focused on Rebula. So Simčič established our region as an important place for winegrowing."

Silvan continues, "It's tough to explain this in terms that sound politically correct today, but he was the Boss. He didn't explain or suggest, he stated. He would let things play up to a certain point, but had a way of gently nudging his colleague to realize that his way was correct. What made him a great leader was that he was truly loved by his employees and by the people of Brda in general." Silvan recalls that, when he was first set to take over as director, Zvonimir said to him, "Ah-ha, you'll be the new director. Hm. How do you think that's going to work out?" It was an informal, but important, interview. He asked Silvan a few key questions: What do you think of the cooperative? What do you think of Klet Brda? What do you think of Rebula? "For me, Rebula is number one," Silvan replied. And that concluded the meeting. Silvan had replied correctly and had the seal of approval from the Boss.

Despite being The Boss, he was down to earth. Claudio Fabbro recalls that "Miro was not a man of spectacle. He was a kind man, and he always kept an eye on the institution. When we entered the cellar at Dobrovo, he was very proud and in his element. When the delegation from Friuli-Venezia-Giulia came, we participated in delegations from Brda or Ljubljana, we never dealt with politics. This was about wine and economics. He said he absolutely would not discuss politics. In this way, we always got along and focused on the wine. He was always smiling at such events. We always had a feeling of camaraderie. That we were one territory in the same business and with the same loves. He always hugged us in greeting and when we left. You left with a sense that he was eager to see you again. Availability, humanity, kindness. He knew that delegates would be a bit timid with their first glass of Rebula in hand. But by the third...everyone was more open, courageous, friendly, switching from the formal to the informal. Our families would spend time together regularly from 1982 on. Like one big family."

Marjan Simčič grew up with Miro as a close friend of his father's. "He was a wonderful person. He was calm, but when he had something to say, he was serious and firm. He knew how to make things happen and he knew how to navigate at the time when he established Klet Brda. He was a strong manager. But back in the day, there were experts and there were managers, and few people were both experts and good managers. He was. We called him 'Medot.' He was complex and had an expertise in many fields."

I spoke to several of Miro's protégés and gathered recollections of what he was like as a boss. "He was rather strict and demanding, like a good teacher." Silvan says. "He would ask you something and if you didn't show a good understanding, then he didn't have much time for you. You had to prove yourself and maintain his faith in you."

Ivan Peršolja, one generation younger than Miro, while Silvan is two, had a similar experience. "At the start, he took a lot of time to speak with each new worker. And when he decided that he could trust you, he trusted you 100%. When I came to Brda from my family farm, I thought I knew wine. But at the start I was in charge of investments. It was tricky work, but he was there to help. For my first fourteen days at the job, he sent me to a seminar in Radenci. He knew that I needed this knowledge base and I returned with many ideas and plans. In that time, we made many investments that worked out very well for us, and at the time this was not straightforward. He had faith in his colleagues, but we could not take that for granted or misuse it. He evaluated the competence and abilities of each worker. If something wasn't clear, he encouraged us to ask, better twice than not at all. But if you lost his trust, that was it. He was a decisive person. Mature. And I'm truly proud of having known him and been a part of his team."

Marjan Četrtič worked for Klet Brda, as did his wife, both in the sales department. "My wife was also working at Klet Brda when I was, and once she complained about our kids in front of Zvonimir. 'They're so hyperactive,' she said. And he replied, 'Be happy about that. It means that they'll make something of themselves.' He had a down-to-earth manner. He was the sort who threw you into the deep end and said, 'Get on with it.' He left us to our own initiatives.

The Klet Brda archive bears a strong imprint of Zvonimir Simčič, as most of the wines stored hail from his era

There was a strict order about who was in charge. If we look at the people just below Zvonimir as director, like the oenologists, there was never a debate—he was in charge. Not that he was authoritarian, but he was an authority, an expert. The key was his having trained in Italy. He acquired knowledge there that others in Yugoslavia didn't have. That was why he was ahead of all the others.

"I first met him when I applied for the job at Klet Brda to be head of sales," Četrtič continues. "That was my first meeting with him, and he hired me. He was a visionary in love with Rebula. The father of Rebula. He was totally in love with it. At the time, this was the most-sold wine in Yugoslavia. The bubbly sort was hugely popular on the market. That has come back, now the market wants these fresh, young wines again.

"At Klet Brda, it was socialist times. It was halfway into capitalistic markets. There was a lot of bureaucracy. We could not regulate the prices based on demand. There was always too little Rebula. We would have liked to have increased the price, but this was controlled from above. Those days it was not hard to sell Rebula, it was hard to decide who would get it. The main public was in Yugoslavia. Zagreb, Belgrade, Sarajevo, but most of all Slovenia."

Many of the locals Miro hired at Klet Brda consider him to be an unofficial godfather to them. For many he was the first to offer proper employment with the opportunity for advancement. Ivan Peršolja, current president of the Slovenian Sommelier's Association, is one. "He hired me, and we got along beautifully. I received a lot of knowledge and experience under his wing, professional and personal. In Slovenia and abroad. When I came to Slovenia interested in being a sommelier I heard about Miro. Back then few people knew what a sommelier is. Right at the start, when I was invited as a member of Farmer's Cooperative, we took a trip to Soave. That was the first time I met a sommelier and saw how they work in person. That really inspired me to train for that role myself. This trip was arranged by Miro."

Another is Klet Brda's long-time secretary, Vili Mišigoj. "Zvonimir Simčič was a man who never did anything with concern for his image," he begins. "He always worked for the benefit of others and the greater good of the region. Since we are on the border, we had a different set of problems from our countrymen in the middle of Slovenia. Many of them we created ourselves, and Engineer Simčič saw them for what they were, and saw the long-term goals. Most people here were very conservative, worried about hunger and working only towards what was immediately relevant to them and their families. He wanted to create something greater and long-lasting to help the region. Considering his abilities and success, Brda farmers saw in him a light of hope for a better future. A chance at better work and more reward. Everyone was in favor of his being the leader of the winery. But at the start, he did not want this. He was nominated three times for the post of director of Klet Brda, but he just wanted to be the oenologist—not the director of the whole operation. The third time, we convinced him to also take on the role of director. But only on the condition that he also remain the oenologist.

"He wasn't interested in business, just in wine. He did not work for his own, personal benefit. He focused on the collective farmers and winemakers. He often said, 'If the farmer is happy, then we will be, too.' And he followed his plan beautifully, from beginning to end. Toward the end of his career, when other experts from the faculty came to lead Klet Brda, he remained a proponent of Rebula and saw to it that Rebula remained the focus of Klet Brda. His main goal was for the farmers to live better. We did not pay for grapes at the harvest, when they brought the grapes to the winery. That's what most wineries did. Instead, we paid after the wine was made and sold. If it sold better, we would pay more to the farmers who had provided the better-selling grapes. In this way, we rewarded the farmers for better produce, when it was clear that their grapes had sold better. He divided the profits among the farmers, the winemakers, and the sellers. This approach was unbelievably positive and new for Yugoslavia. We set up our own bank, Hranilno Kreditno Službo, and through this the farmers were in charge of their own bank. When Simčič was director, if he saw something, he would develop it. He saw how to stimulate each person in the wine-making process and did so. The whole operation was pulled forward by Engineer Simčič's good character. He was there to succeed, and he saw farther than others.

Even the current, long-standing mayor of Goriška Brda, Franc Mužič, got his start working under Miro at Klet Brda. He is a man of great energy, charm, and dynamism, with the natural charisma of a beloved politician. He has done great things to promote Goriška Brda as a tourist destination and wine center, helping to move it far up the "Monopoly board."

"Rebula and Zvonimir Simčič mean an enormous amount for Goriška Brda. Without a doubt, Rebula is the variety best associated with Brda. Our parents and grandparents cultivated it. The official first reference to it in documentation is from around 1340. For centuries it has been associated with this region. Simčič was my director when I was a young man working for Klet Brda. That was during Yugoslavia and even when, in principle, everyone was a 'comrade' at the same level, Simčič was, for me, always someone I called 'Sir.' A man of great authority and ability. He always knew the best way forward to achieve an optimal outcome. He was director of Klet Brda for 16 or 17 years and was the lead oenologist for many years more. He established Klet Brda in 1957 and it is a great success to this day. During his time, there were more than 1000 collaborators in the Brda area who worked with Klet Brda and under the supervision of Simčič. We can say that around 80% of the grapes in our region went through Klet Brda. Later, when Slovenia was independent, these numbers shifted, of course, but still around 40% of the region's grapes are made into wine at Klet Brda. Simčič established the platform that led to its success.

"I was young at the time," Mayor Franc Mužič continues, "I led two divisions at the winery, as I was specialized in technical matters and oversaw transport. I was in charge of some 50 people who worked with the cooperative. Most of them were younger, aside from a few drivers. Simčič was always the ultimate gentleman and the exemplar in business and personal interactions. He was a person of true authority. He knew how to handle and fix any problem. He was also versed in navigating the complexities of the Yugoslav system, with frequent changes in required business methods. He also had good people around him and knew who to trust. I can say without doubt that we were one of the best businesses in Yugoslavia and the exemplar to others. People came from throughout Yugoslavia to learn from what we built.

"The first meeting was when I was hired through the cooperative. I led an independent mechanical workshop before working under Simčič, with some 15 people employed. And we joined forces with a mechanical workshop to work as a team at Klet Brda, through the Kmetijska Zadruga Goriška Brda (the Farmer's Cooperative of Goriška Brda), where Simčič was director. We handled transport. But I had heard good things about him for many years, when he was director of Klet Brda (he was later director of the entire Farmer's Cooperative). He was the author of the whole concept of Klet Brda. After independence, Klet Brda survived and there was talk of shifting to a Russian-style system of centralized ownership, and I agreed that this was not the way forward. I ensured that Klet Brda remains Slovene, and it is still an exemplar of business practice, now in independent Slovenia. Zvonimir Simčič was the exemplar of good leadership in business, and we continue the approach he established.

"As a director...and I see this as mayor, too...you need to know how to navigate experiences at various levels, including the level of conflict. When I encounter some sort of problem in my current position, I'll often think back on how Zvonimir handled such situations and I draw inspiration from it. He had a trick that was important for all parties to feel that they had been heard, their opinions and concerns voiced. Say there was an issue in my department at the Klet. Someone would come to complain. He would just listen at first. Then he would say, 'Okay, now we've heard your thoughts on the matter. Now let's hear from Franc.' He made it clear that everyone's opinion was valid, and he would hear all sides of an issue, before making an executive decision about how best to handle it."

A common refrain among memories of Miro is how he empowered his staff. This was not common in Yugoslavia, where the most common approach to leadership was strict authoritarianism. Giving power to those beneath you was not the done thing. Miro was particularly modern in his approach.

Mužič continues, "He built Rebula in quality, as a brand, and he handled the politics required to make this happen during Yugoslavia. Even the name, Rebula, he established. But I'll always remember that moment when he mediated an argument I was having with the Secretary of the Farmer's Cooperative, who was in a superior position to me, and said, 'Now we have to hear what Franc has to say.' That made me feel that I was an equal and that he was giving us equal weight, not regarding the professional position and hierarchy. This was unusual for the time, and I try to continue this approach to leadership."

* * * * *

Silvan had known who Miro was, of course, but never met him until he was already director of Klet Brda. One day, Miro showed up at his office. Silvan recalled that he only realized after Miro had entered what the meeting was going to be about. Miro was now sizing up Silvan inside his former office, and he wanted to be sure that Klet Brda was in the right hands.

Thankfully for all involved, Miro wholeheartedly approved of Silvan and the two became friends. Miro passed on advice, for instance how he'd always been careful to maintain a distance between himself and the staff of Klet Brda, ensuring that he remained the authority figure. He was always kind, courteous, and correct but he rarely joined them on staff excursions and such. He once described to Silvan that the cooperative was always riding the line between democracy and anarchy. This might sound odd, since it was long functioning during socialism, but it was originally developed as a democratic liberation of 38 families, all farmers from Brda, who together bought 230 hectares of land from the local nobility. It was the end of a feudal approach and the start of a collective, empowering the workers. Marx would have approved (well, at least of part of it). But the trouble with a cooperative of equals is that it risks getting nowhere. Leaders can be useful. "If you listen to everyone," Zvonimir advised Silvan, "you'll get nowhere. Avoid populism."

"In the 50s," Silvan recalls, "when people were leaving Brda, there was a total focus on growing cherries. Other fruit, including grapes, were put aside. When the winery was developed, there was a sense of 'If we're going to win, we've got to go all-in. We have to win and we're going to win with wine.' And so all of Brda focused on the best possible grapes. Brda cherries remained, for farmers, what they thought of as their best seller, but from this point on, the most energy, the most time, the best land was dedicated to grapes. Every farmer had to be in on the plan. One way or another, we were going to change our country and make an imprint on the world."

After independence in 1991, most Slovenian wineries were privatized. Individual owners were pushing to expand to the export market. Zvonimir, long retired by then, saw that independent Slovenia, which was not able to rely on the rest of Yugoslavia, since they'd just been at war for that independence, was too small a market to sustain Klet Brda. It was export or bust.

* * * * *

We toured the facilities, which include a museum exhibit and timeline of wine cultivation in the region, from the ancients through Count de Baguer and on to 1954, when Klet Brda was founded (the cylindrical cellar was built in 1955 and the first crop of grapes arrived in 1957, leading to the first vintage, 850,000 liters), finishing in the present. It is interesting that the museum exhibit proudly announces the Klet Brda slogan as "Devoted to Rebula since 1957." That could just as well be Miro's epitaph.

The first oenologists were imported: French consultants brought in to oversee wine production, while the business directors of Klet Brda were political appointees with little to no

Klet Brda remains the largest producer and exporter of wines in Slovenia

Beautiful sunset over Brda/Collio

experience with wine and from outside of the Brda area. The first wine labels were likewise meant to look like French labels, with the first Cabernet sold under the name "Chateau de Dobrovo." The first Rebula had a label bearing the charming incorrect English "Produced of Yugoslavia." Miro was the first Yugoslav oenologist and would take over as business director, as well, in 1968, serving until 1982. The export market began in 1958 with a large order sent to East Germany. The first vintage of sparkling wine was sold in 1962, thanks to Miro's special interest in how to make Rebula into a "champagne." He wanted to use the slow and tricky method preferred by the big names from Champagne, but he had quotas to fill and finite resources, so instead he used the quicker and cheaper approach to Proseccos, the Charmat method, in which the bubbles are introduced through a second fermentation in steel pressure tanks. Many of the wines, particularly the Rebulas, were labeled as "Briška Rebula" (Rebula from Brda). On the one hand this was branding to promote the locality, on the other it was a nod to the playful rivalry with nearby top terroir, Vipava, which produced their own Rebula.

In the midst of Miro's tenure as director, in 1975, Klet Brda was expanded to have the capacity to receive 1500 wagonloads of grapes at a time and producing over 4.4 million liters a year, of which some two-thirds was Rebula. The most the winery has ever produced in a year was 16 million liters, with millions of kilos of grapes processed. That was at a time, in the 70s, when all of Yugoslavia was the market, and Klet Brda was the epitome of efficiency and quality. Delegates from throughout Yugoslavia would travel here to learn and bring the knowledge back to their own industries in the various republics.

This made Miro among the most influential directors in Yugoslavia, regardless of industry. There were some key elements that Silvan sees as Miro's contribution to the Yugoslav business environment, setting aside for a moment the characteristics of the wine itself. First, he had an absolute focus on quality. The product should lead. Always. Clever marketing ploys are fine but are quickly forgotten. They can compel someone to buy a product once, but unless they love the product, they won't buy it again. The idea that quantity can run hand in hand with quality was not self-evident at the time.

We've already mentioned the focus on Rebula, but the idea that a Yugoslav brand should proudly focus on a regional specialty, rather than simply chasing global trends, was also new and revolutionary for Miro's fellow directors of state-run firms throughout the seven republics.

Next, he took good care of not only his staff but the wider network of people who made Klet Brda tick. The farmers in the region never felt like second-class citizens. They worked alongside the staff from Klet Brda, and still to this day there are specially trained technicians who go and visit the 400 farms that grow grapes for Klet Brda and advise them on all aspects of viticulture. Miro thought as a farmer would, considering what they had (one of the world's best terroirs and a strong, proud work ethic) and what they didn't have (equipment, cutting edge know-how), and tried to provide for them. As recently as the 70s, Brda farmers still harvested grapes by hand and placed them in wicker baskets strapped to their backs. The photos from the 70s could easily be mistaken for photos from the 1920s or even earlier.

It was only during the 1960s that Brda farmers slowly shifted away from using yoked animals for agricultural cultivation and began to use tractors. It was difficult to get proper, state of the art farming equipment, fertilizer, and the like, so Miro set up a store adjacent to Klet Brda where the farmers could acquire such items (which were otherwise almost completely unavailable) and could do so at a heavily subsidized rate. The State also determined the quota of equipment that each municipality was allotted: only so many tractors, so many trucks, and so on. Miro was able to convince the powers-that-be to provide the farming equipment needed, far exceeding the quota for Brda. He also bought high-quality equipment, built to last. "He brought in tractors from Italy around 1970," Silvan jokes, "and the same ones he bought still run for us today."

But while modernization, getting up to the races with a V12 engine race car, was a priority, there were optimization techniques that Miro avoided. He preferred hand-picked grapes that traveled in wicker rather than plastic, because grapes would be crushed during the transfer between plastic containers and touching plastic for too long could lead to spoilage. Miro devised a sort of gondola system in which grapes direct from the farmers' wagons could be winched up into the winery with a minimal number of transfers from container to container (each of which would result in a percentage of prematurely crushed grapes).

Miro's connection to, and training in, Italy also opened up new technologies and ways of thinking that businessmen who never left Yugoslavia would not have encountered. For instance, in acquiring and cultivating young vines, Miro looked to Rauscedo, a village at the foot of the Carnic Alps, which was renowned for its grapevine nurseries, Vivai Cooperativi Rauscedo, founded in 1933, which employed a special technique called "bench-grafting." By

1948, this village was producing 3 million grafted vine cuttings a year that were in demand by winemakers the world over. This was the cradle for the vines planted at Klet Brda.

And the Rebula vines at Klet Brda were the cradle for the wine industry in Yugoslavia and the eventual international recognition of the variety.

* * * * *

Klet Brda manages still to be both the largest wine producer in Slovenia and one that produces a boutique level of quality. This is hard to do. The man who ensures that quality today, and has for the last thirty years, is Darinko Ribolica. Yes, that's actually his name, people. *Nomen est omen*, as they say. He is the world's foremost authority of Rebula/Ribolla Gialla, the literal and figurative inheritor of Miro's mantle, and his surname suggests that he isn't the first member of his family to hold such a title.

"Rebula is perfectly suited to this terroir," Darinko told me, as we sat with Eldina for a tasting of all of Klet Brda's Rebula options. "Naturally, since this is where it comes from. Miro knew that the best this terroir could produce was what was native to it. But it's not easy to grow. It requires sun. It requires this sort of land. It requires shale. And it requires the sort of people who know how to cultivate it. In my opinion, Miro's greatest vision was seeing the potential in Rebula."

It turns out that, while 2020 was a year to forget for many things, it will be a year to remember for Rebula. "It was the best harvest of Rebula I can recall," Darinko confirms. It was an early, or "green harvest," but the quality of the grapes was at a level Darinko has never before seen. That's a good sign for the bottles that will be for sale a few years from now.

Darinko's laboratory is located in the original Klet Brda building, with its striking cylindrical design. As an art historian with a PhD in the history of architecture, I'm naturally drawn to this building, which is reminiscent of the Guggenheim in New York at first glance. While it doesn't contain a helicoidal ramp inside, it has the air of a building created with both form and function in mind. When we step into Darinko's office, he has a selection of reds in sample-sized glass bottles laid out on his desk. I make a mental note that, in my next life, I should do my best to become Darinko. Tasting wine all day, creating, in love with what you do, and renowned for your authority. Sounds good to me.

We adjourn to an elegant tasting room adjacent to the winery. Darinko walks us through a tasting for four Rebulas. Now, you may well have been to wine tastings, but there's something special about the vibe when your guide is the man who actually designed the wine. It's like going to an art gallery, let's say the Guggenheim, and having the artist in question as your docent. That's a level up from someone simply pointing out the tasting notes you should look for ("yeast, fresh brioche, peaches") because now you can hear about the thought process behind the design of each wine.

First up was Quercus Rebula, the entry level of Klet Brda. But there's nothing entry level about it, other than the price. I've heard from a number of friends that they consider the Quercus line from Klet Brda, launched in 2000, to be by far the best quality-to-price ratio on the market. Bottles cost around 5 Euros, but you wouldn't guess that in a pricetag-less tasting. "With this wine we established a standard," begins Darinko as we sip, "one that other wineries abide by. For all the best-selling, trendy Rebulas, Quercus is the standard baseline to which others are compared, and it's an extremely high point of departure." The idea is that the bar set high means that other Rebulas will be obliged to go even higher. If this is the inexpensive everyday Rebula (Darinko thinks it should cost more, but Silvan wants to keep it accessible to all), and it's this good, then other vintners must necessarily shoot for the stars with their Rebula offerings. "If you want to know how Rebula in opoka soil should be, this is where you should begin."

In such a wine-focused area, Darinko's family was perhaps the most wine-focused of all, going back generations. They also knew how to party, hosting gatherings frequently. But it was considered something of an oddity, back in the 1920s, that the Ribolica clan preferred wine over beer. "I come from a family that has always been involved in wine," Darinko says, as he pours the next sample. "My grandfather was one of the original founders of the cooperative in 1922, when this was still part of Italy. That was when a group of Brda families got together to buy some land from Count de Baguer. It's easy to forget that the cooperative, which we tend to associate with socialism, began long before that period, when this area was Italian." Wine expertise is in the Ribolica DNA. And they always liked the good stuff. Back when buying wine cheaply and for quantity was the default, his family were noted for buying by the bottle. "Our door was open to anyone who wished to come and visit, provided they brought with them a

The Bagueri line from Klet Brda is one of their top offerings

bottle of wine. That was the ticket into our home." Then the reputation spread that you'd drink well at the Ribolica homestead, and so it became a favorite gathering spot.

Next, we dipped into something completely different, but still a Rebula. The Krasno Rebula. The name is a play on words, because the *Kras* is the Slovenian for Karst terrain, but *krasno* means "charming" or "lovely." The scent would have made me think we had shifted to a totally different grape. Fresher, grassier, sharper. "This is made in a different principle from Quercus," Darinko explains. "The grapes are selected as you would a Grand Cru." They are harvested 2-3 weeks after those destined for Quercus. Then lightly macerated and fermented in giant barrels. "It's a different concept. Rebula's other face." The variety of what Rebula can be is part of why experts like Darinko enjoy working with it. "It offers a broad palette of possibilities," he says. "Because it has acidity and low alcohol, it works well as a sparkling wine. Because it's fruity and fresh, as in Quercus, it takes on wood nicely. It ages well and functions as a more serious wine, if you want it to. I've often heard that, alongside Chardonnay, Rebula is the only white that is really a good compliment to meats. It has enough character."

Darinko has tried aging in all manners of wooden barrels: acacia, chestnut, cherry... Farmers in the region used to employ acacia and chestnut primarily, since it was what was most readily available. But he always comes back to oak, preferably French. The other woods provided dimensions that overpowered the grape. Oak is the least intrusive, the most subtle.

If Quercus is the line of Rebula wines at Klet Brda that have the best price-performance ration, then the Bagueri line is for special occasions. Turns out the Italianization of the name (Bagueri, not Baguer) was simply a legal issue. When Klet Brda first launched the line, in 1991, the year of Slovenia's independence, contacting and getting permission from the de Baguer family was not feasible, and so they opted for a name that recalled the local Count, but which would not cause any issues.

As soon as I sniffed the Bagueri Rebula, I was hit with the primary note that had haunted me since the Masterclass tasting. It is a buttery wine. I'd like to be more diverse in my comments, but while I may be a writer, what I can express about wine remains at novice level. The umami/butter/truffle concept is what I've felt with all of the best Rebula wines. The Krasno I'd just tried was an interesting exception—I liked it very much, it just didn't taste "Rebulish," to coin a new term.

Motnik is the result of Darinko's special project, to bring back
the wine of our ancestors

Bagueri is Klet Brda's high-end brand, A-level wine (although they recently launched an A+ label called, well, A+). The grapes come from the four farms among the 400 that serve the winery that Darinko considers the best. Darinko will visit these top four farms ten times a year personally.

Now Darinko leans in to reveal a trick of the trade, a secret weapon in his arsenal. "I have a database that is broader and deeper than any I know," he confides. "I have exact information about harvest, farms, and vintages for the last twenty-five years. This makes the selection of grapes much easier." Two full-time specialists circulate among the farms, advising and testing and tasting and maintaining this elaborate database, which takes the guesswork out of knowing which grapes should go into which bottles. This comes in handy. "Working with 400 farmers is not easy. Standing beside the 400 farmers," Darinko jokes, "are 400 farmers' wives, which is really not easy." But Darinko's authority in Brda is a close approximation to what Miro enjoyed. Everyone knows that Darinko knows best, and they are happy to accept his advice.

Darinko saved a special treat for the climax, which he mentions is his "life project," and Silvan and Simon joined us just in time. "History always fascinated me. I briefly flirted with being an archaeologist." Eldina and I start laughing because we, too, each wanted to be Indiana Jones at some point in our lives. "In 2005, I was reading a book by ethnologist Pavel Medvešček about antique methods of preparing Black Rebula in the village of Zgorna Brda." Darinko's eyes sparkled as he described his special barrels, four of which he keeps as a private lab where he can experiment. He grew interested in Pokalca/Schiopettino, a hyper-local version that has been called *črna Rebula,* Black Rebula. If Rebula is the golden wine, I joke, then we might call Pokalca "black gold." Darinko's love of history and his homeland made him wish to resurrect the lost methods of his ancestors, and here was an authentic recipe to follow. "First they smoked the barrels with gently burning herbs. Then they'd seal the interior and repeat this process several more times. Come September they would crush the grapes and leave the juice in those barrels until the following spring." This created a special wine they called Motnik, which we might translate as "cloudy" because, as Darinko suggests, "it was difficult to make it clear, due to all the smoked and herbal components." The smoking process sounds unusual, but Darinko thinks that this was the best way they had to sterilize the barrels. "When I read that, we decided to reproduce this recipe and use it with Rebula."

The recipe called for some elements that sounded odd, like chestnut tree resin. The first time he tried it, it was less than appealing. "The result was *merda*," he jokes. The main suspect was the resin, which was, well, too resin-y (as you might imagine, discernably unpleasant to taste and to smell). "Some people like this. The ancient Greeks supposedly did. It's not for me," he smiles. "So we cut out his ingredient. In 2006, we started to use the herbs in different quantities than the recipe called for. The bay leaf was too dominant, the rosemary. But I was carried away with this project, my colleagues and our wives, as well." They produced only four barrels and did so off-the-record, as an after-hours hobby. But word spread around Klet Brda and in the Brda wine circles that Darinko was up to something interesting. "In 2011, we were obliged to go public," he smiles proudly. The wine was so good, so distinctive, that Silvan insisted, and it became a boutique offering from a colossus of a winery.

Motnik was certainly the most complex and interesting served in this flight ("This is a wine for meditation," Darinko says), but I was particularly taken with it since its inventor sat before us, bubbling with delight as he told its story and sipped his creation.

At this point, prior to lunch, I'd been a good boy. I reasoned that I didn't really have to spit out the wine, which seemed both a shame and was still slightly gross from my perspective, if I took mini, mini, mini sips. The problem was that the wine was so good that I took many, many, many mini, mini, mini sips. Good thing that I didn't have to drive home for hours.

8
TASTING
GORIŠKA
BRDA AND
COLLIO

TASTING GORIŠKA BRDA AND COLLIO

If you haven't already, I bet that you're keen to do a tasting tour of your own in this beautiful slice of our planet. I had the good fortune of tasting my way through fifteen Rebula wines at the Masterclass, and if you can finagle yourself an invitation, you can, too. But Goriška Brda is a wonderful spot for a holiday, as we'll see shortly. And what better backbone to a holiday than tasting your way through a region?

There are many ways to do this. If you're planning a visit in person then you'll likely want to approach your tasting tour in some logical order by location. Have a look at our map to see who is based where. But for our purposes, this short chapter on tasting notes, focusing on the vintners who produce Rebula and are part of the Masterclass, I've included various types of Rebula wine: classic, matured, extended skin contact (a.k.a. "orange wine"), and sparkling.

By now, I've learned enough to know that I know very little—someone once said that this is the sign of a wise man. Truly understanding sparkling wine requires a whole different level than my introductory dip into this world. There are so many different factors at play, and one must work within the context of the world's dominant idea of sparkling wine being strictly lashed to champagne. I've already mentioned sparkling wine made with the Charmat method out of 100% Rebula grapes, similar to Prosecco. There are, indeed, splendid examples of it, like those made by Klet Brda or Collavini in Italy. But if I were to point you to the specific taste of the terroir, when it comes to sparkling wine, I would go for a classic method wine. These, for me, best represent masterpieces of this terroir, and I'm particularly partial to those based on Rebula, like Medot.

For this chapter, I chose to feature wines that are primarily made from Rebula, favoring those that are 100% Rebula, and sparkling wines made with the classic method. Have a look at my favorite vintners and consider visiting them all. Or, if time is tight, head over to the House of Rebula at Dobrovo Castle, which is the best spot to taste almost all of them without having to rise from your chair.

If orange Rebula is a confusing concept in a book called *Gold Wine,* then you'll just have to sip one of Joško Gravner's potions. Gravner is described as the mad scientist of the region—he is inevitably termed a genius, he does his own thing, he doesn't pay attention to marketing and sales, he charges more and still sells out of all he can make. He is the intellectual wine lover's vintner. The wine equivalent to Russian director Andrei Tarkovsky in film history.

Beloved of the artsy types, perhaps less known by the general public, but those in the know place his wine in its own category.

When it comes to Rebula, he likes to macerate the grapes in enormous terracotta amphorae sealed with beeswax—so large that you could squeeze two people inside them, provided they were very flexible and comfortable with intimacy. This is how wine was stored in the ancient world. "My goal was merely to simplify things," he said. "People have been making wine this way for five thousand years. The amphora, handmade from clay of the Caucasus, is the perfect container for fermenting wine, like a mother's womb." And the result is a wine that is orange-ish in color. Just don't call it orange in front of Gravner.

"Amber captures life, in the form of organic matter, and it's desirable in a natural wine. Orange is a sign of excessive oxidation, and the delicate fruit expression of the terroir is lost. Rebula is an amber wine, not an orange one!"

Okay, let's go with amber, then. The color is down to a six-to-seven month snuggle with the grape skin on inside those amphorae. The amphorae are buried in the earth with only the necks exposed. It's bottled only after five-to-seven years and comes out cloudy, without filtration. It's different, ingenious, a little weird, a lot wonderful. Recall my tasting notes from the Masterclass after sipping a 2009 Gravner Rebula: "liquefied leather wallet." But in the best possible way. To be honest, it was the most mind-blowing I tried, because it didn't really taste like any of the others, or even like wine. It was more whiskey-ish. But man, was it good.

Refreshingly, Gravner isn't interested in catering to the public. He's doing his own thing. And as with all geniuses doing something to perfection, the knowledgeable public comes to him.

The wineries mentioned are those that are affiliated with the annual Rebula Masterclass or that wanted to speak with me for this book about Miro. This is, therefore, a personal selection and there are many more excellent wineries in the Brda/Collio region to try out. Sure, you could come here for a one-week tasting holiday. Or why not just move here?

Let's start with extended skin contact (don't call hem orange)...We'll also include some of my favorites that would be categorized as classic, matured and sparkling. I prefer those that are 100% Rebula or close to it.

Gravner
Oslavia, Italy
Since 1901
15 hectares of vineyards
Approximately 34,000 bottles produced per year

Ribolla
Buried in Georgian kvevri amphorae, fermented
with natural yeast on the skins for 5-6 months,
then for the same period in the kvevri without
skins. Oak barrel aged for six years, bottle aged
for at least 6 months.

Joško Gravner, Gravner

Radikon
Oslavia, Italy
Since 1979
15 hectares of vineyards
Approximately 35,000 bottles produced per year

Ribolla
Macerated for 90 days with skin, then oak barrel
aged for five years, then bottle aged for 18 months.

Saša Radikon, Radikon

Erzetič
Višnjevik, Slovenia
Since 1725
15 hectares of vineyards
Approximately 70,000 bottles produced per year

Here you can taste classic Rebula, but also a
wonderful example of extended skin contact wine:

Amfora Belo
Approximately 2000 bottles produced per year
Grapes are pressed after 7 months of maceration
in amphorae. They are then barrique matured
for 18 months on fine lees, followed by at least
6 months of bottle maturation.

Andrej Erzetič, Erzetič

Kristian Keber
Zegla, Cormons, Italy
Since 2011
1.7 hectares of vineyards
Approximately 2500 bottles produced per year

This special wine, based on Rebula,
is named after the region:

Brda
One-month maceration in cement with stalks,
no temperature control and indigenous yeasts.
Two years of maturation in oak barrels, followed
by one year in the bottle.

Kristian Keber, Keber

Moro
Vipolže, Slovenia
Since 2004
7 hectares of vineyards
Approximately 40,000 bottles produced per year

Here you will find a great example of extended
skin contact Rebula:

Rebula Margherita
Grapes are placed in cases after the harvest for
one month (usually harvested mid-September and
dried until mid-October). They are then pressed.
Fermentation is done with selected yeast in
stainless steel at 18 degrees Celsius. After
fermentation, the wine is placed in a Clayver
for 10 months.

Boris Jakončič, Moro

Klet Brda
Dobrovo, Slovenia
Since 1957
1000 hectares of vineyards
Approximately 6,000,000 bottles produced per year

To taste is sparkling Rebula made with
the Charmat method, try also De Baguer Motnik –
single wineyard, made with an ancient method.
For classic Rebula, try Quercus, while Klet Brda's
matured options include Krasno or Bagueri,
which is my favorite:

Rebula Bagueri
Approximately 30,000 bottles produced per year
Fermented and matured part in large barrels
and part in barrique, followed by 6 months
of bottle maturation.

Darinko Ribolica, Klet Brda

Ščurek

Plešivo, Slovenia

Since the 1890s

21 hectares of vineyards

Approximately 100,000 bottles produced per year

Among their splendid cuvee wines, including
Rebula, they offer also:

Rumena Rebula (Yellow Rebula)
Approximately 10,000 bottles produced per year
Cold macerated in a wine press for 8 hours,
followed by soft pressure with a pneumatic wine
press and static decantation of must. Fermented
in Inox barrels at 8 degrees Celsius. Matured for
5 months in the lees in stainless steel tanks, bottle
aged for at least one month.

Tomaž Ščurek, Ščurek

Dolfo
Ceglo, Slovenia
Since 1909
14 hectares of vineyards
Approximately 55,000 bottles produced per year

Here you will find a great example
of classic Rebula:

Rumena Rebula (Yellow Rebula)
Approximately 4000 bottles produced per year
Five hours of maceration, skin contact
fermentation at less than 24 degrees Celsius.
Regular punching down of the cap with light
pumping over. Use of indigenous yeast only. After
pressing, fermentation continues in stainless steel
tanks, with the lees stirred regularly until the first
decanting. Matured for 10 months in steel tanks
and at least 8 months in the bottle.

Marko Skočaj, Dolfo

Zanut

Neblo, Slovenia

Since 1976

8 hectares of vineyards

Approximately 50,000 bottles produced per year

Zanut offers a fine classic Rebula:

Rebula

Approximately 3300 bottles produced per year
Cold macerated for 24 hours, pressed, then
fermented in stainless steel tanks for 30-35 days
at 15 degrees Celsius. Matured for 11 months in
stainless steel tanks, followed by 6 months bottle
maturation.

Borut Kocijančič, Zanut

Medot

Dobrovo, Slovenia

Since 1812

3.5 hectares of vineyards

Approximately 27,000 bottles produced per year

They are known for sparkling Rebula-based wines,
but they have introduced this classic Rebula
in loving memory of the life journey
of Zvonimir Simčič:

Rebula Journey

Half of the hand-harvested grapes are
immediately pressed, cooling the must at
8 degrees Celsius in stainless-steal. After two days,
the process continues with racking and
the addition of selected yeasts. Fermentation
takes place at a maximum of 16 degrees Celsius.
The remaining grapes are cold macerated for
48 hours then gentled pressed and fermented at
a slightly higher temperature. They are then aged
on lees from October through April and the
two wines are combined and bottled in May.
Three-month bottle maturation.

Simon Simčič, Medot

Jermann
Dolegna del Collio, Italy
Since 1881
160 hectares of vineyards
Approximately 900,000 bottles produced per year

Their remarkable cuvee wines include
a matured Rebula:

Višvik
Approximately 4000 bottles produced per year
Three days of cold maceration followed
by fermentation in 750-liter Slavonian oak barrels.
Matured in oak barrels for 8 months, followed
by one year in the bottle.

Silvio Jermann, Jermann

Edi Simčič
Vipolže, Slovenia
Since 1989
12 hectares of vineyards
Approximately 50,000 bottles produced per year

Taste a classic Rebula and a wonderful example
of a matured version, made from a single
39-year-old vineyard:

Rebula Fojana
Barrel fermented for 10 months on lees.
Matured in oak barrels for 10 months, followed
by at least 6 months in the bottle.

Aleks Simčič, Edi Simčič

Marjan Simčič
Ceglo, Slovenia
Since 1860
20 hectares of vineyards
Approximately 100,000 bottles produced per year

Marjan Simčič offers many Rebula-based wines:
Classic, Cru and Opoka Cru. Leonardo is a sweet
version, with sugar created by drying the grapes.
My favorite of his Rebulas is:

Ribolla Opoka
Approximately 3000 bottles produced per year
Skin contact fermentation for 14 days in 1000-liter
concrete eggs. Softly pressed with pneumatic
pressure. 12-month maturation in concrete eggs
followed by 10 months in 500-liter oak barrels.
Bottle matured for at least 4 months.

Marjan Simčič, Marjan Simčič

Ferdinand
Kojsko, Slovenia
Since 1997
6 hectares of vineyards
Approximately 30,000 bottles produced per year

Ferdinand offers Rebula Classic, Rebula Época
and, my favorite, Rebula Brutus. If you visit, make
sure to ask about a special cross border joint
classic sparkling wine project that was developed
with Italian colleague, Robert Prinčič
(of Gradis'ciutta), called Sinefinis Rebollium.

Ribolla Gialla Brutus
Grapes are destemmed into barrels where berries
are left in the must that begins spontaneous
fermentation with a wild indigenous yeast culture.
After fermentation, the barrels are refilled, and
the berries are left in contact with the wine until
the next harvest (so for 12 months). Only then is
the wine separated from the berries and further
matured in barrels for another year. The wine is
bottled unfiltered.

Matjaž Četrtič, Ferdinand

Movia

Ceglo, Slovenia

Since 1820

22 hectares of vineyards

Approximately 100,000 bottles produced per year

A visit to this house is an unforgettable experience. You will be able to try Rebula different vintages, Veliko Rebula – which means "grand Rebula" - and very special, Lunar - Moon. The most remarkable experience is opening a bottle of Puro sparkling, special in that it is not disgorged, so the bottles are opened upside down in the bowl of water. Just opening a bottle is an event itself:

Puro Amber

Grapes are destemmed and macerated for 14 days, after which the must is pressed. When the must has naturally cleared, fermentation begins in Inox tanks and is finished in French oak barrique barrels, where the wine spends one year. The base wine is then bottled with approximately 7% must from the current year's harvest, which is used during the classic method process (we do not use liqueur d'expedition).

Aleš Kristančič, Movia

Silveri

Neblo, Slovenia

Since 1710

3.5 hectares of vineyards

Approximately 20,000 bottles produced per year

Here you will find a classic Rebula and a sparkling
wine made of 100% Rebula:

Blanc de Blancs

A combination of three different Rebula grapes
(50% from the Muško vineyard, 30% from the
Gmajna vineyard, 20% from the Vrh vineyard).
Vinification after the first fermentation in steel
tanks. Matured on yeasts for 36 months.

Tadej and Taras Gašparin, Silveri

Gradis'Ciutta

San Floriano del Collio, Italy

Since 1997

40 hectares of vineyards

Approximately 200,000 bottles produced per year

Gradis'Ciutta offers a very nice example of mature
Rebula, but we should not forget their cross
border joint classic sparkling wine project
developed with Slovenian colleague, Matjaž Četrtič
(of Ferdinand), called Sinefinis Rebollium.

Sveti Nikolaj Rebula

Approximately 3300 bottles produced per year
Aged for 9 months in large Slavonian oak barrels,
it is then further matured in the bottle for
12 months.

Robert Prinčič, Gradis'ciutta

9

GORIŠKA
BRDA
IS WORTH
A JOURNEY

GORIŠKA BRDA IS WORTH A JOURNEY

It is not lost on me that this observation tower, little more than a concrete spiral staircase, resembles a corkscrew. It's hypnotic, torqueing my way up twist after twist, but oh, man, what a view at the top. The tower is the most popular spot for tourists in Goriška Brda, and from its summit you can see, weather permitting, the Julian Alps to the north, the Bay of Venice to the west (just 90 minutes away), and endless hills covered in vines that recall Tuscany more than Middle Europe. In fact, those terraced hills are so special that the process is underway to get them UNESCO heritage status. To the east, I can see the stone promontory known as Nanos, an imposing monolithic hill that Herodotus wrote about, calling it the barrier between the Alps and the Mediterranean. Turns out this is not just a historical saying. As geologist and wine specialist Denis Rusjan confirms, "Historians used to write things for a reason, after generations of observation. When we drive from Ljubljana towards Primorska, Nanos is really a sort of barrier and there's a shift in the weather as we pass it." As Herodotus would have said, Nanos blocks the icy winds tumbling down from the Alps, and blocks the warmer, salt-sea air from the Adriatic, bottling these two meteorological zones into a region that is, quite simply, wine central, with Goriška Brda and the nearby Vipava Valley considered among the top terroirs in the world.

First, let it be said that Goriška Brda is a place, not a town or even a village. To be clear, it is a cluster of villages that share this special terroir, opoka in Slovenian or flysch in fancy, scientific English. It is comprised of 45 villages spread over 72 square kilometers, the largest of which are Dobrovo, Šmartno and Gonjače. But none are exactly large (Gonjače has a population of 190). What unifies them is the terroir, and that carries over across the artificial border with Italy into the Italian region known as Collio. This was a single region, from the time of the Roman Empire through to the Second World War, when the border was inserted in the middle of an area that thought of itself as one unified place. The feeling of unification is still so great that Goriška Brda and Collio launched a cross-border initiative for a joint brand, in order to emphasize the origin, nature, and quality of Rebula/Ribolla Gialla from this region—a rare such case in the EU.

This is a unique landscape, a political and geographical point of union between Germanic, Romantic, and Slavic peoples and cultures. And the top of the observation tower is the perfect place to understand it.

Gonjače observation tower

The entirety of Šmartno village has been declared a cultural heritage monument

The climate is Mediterranean, despite the cooling loom of the Alps, and this is a happy place for fruit and vegetables. The connection to fruit is evident from a quick glance at a map, with many of Brda's villages named after what was harvested there: Figovica (figs, *fige*), Višnjevik (sour cherries, *višnje*), Hruševlje (pears, *hruške*). Scanning the landscape, we can still see the legacy of ancient Roman agricultural strategies: planting fruit orchards, crops, and grapevines together, in groups on terraces called *brajda* locally. Romans knew that vines thrived when growing alongside other fruit, which created a "living support."

From the observation tower, I head to the Tourist Information Center in the village of Šmartno. Tourism is exceptionally well-run here, and the info center brims with local specialties for sale and a helpful map suggesting a Top Five sites to see in the area. I'm careful to distinguish sites to see from things to do, because there is really one thing that tourists and Slovenians (and Italians) come here to do: to taste wine. Ask any Slovenian or north-eastern Italian what Goriška Brda is known for, and they will say wine and cherries. This was the cherry basket of the Austro-Hungarian Empire—literally. It was the only claim to fame for what was otherwise an impoverished, agricultural community of charming but unimportant villages. They produced great sour cherries, consumed with delight from Vienna to Budapest, but that was about it. Thanks to the introduction of a railroad, the cherries were eventually exported to such far-flung places as Galicia, Saxony, and Lvov. Is the *opoka* soil that allows vines to flourish here also particularly good for sour cherries? As geologist Denis Rusjan notes, "I'm not a fruit specialist, but from a plant angle, both use a deep root system, pulling up water from deeper in the earth. Maybe that's why both do well here. Cherries grow on trees with roots that are many meters long, so it is prepared for drought and can last well." This is a heavenly place for fruit with deep root systems that thrives when it lightly suffers, producing the best possible produce.

A later cash crop was prunes: specifically peeled, dried plums treated with Sulphur dioxide as a preservative were produced here, referred to as *prunella,* and exported as far as North America. But still, a region cannot live on seasonal cherries and prunes alone. Wine was made here, and has been for millennia, but it was not distinguished or recognized abroad, nor was it an industry, just local families making it for mostly local consumption, until the arrival of Count Silverij de Baguer, the 19th-century hero of the region, who led to the 20th-century protagonist, Miro Simčič.

From the observation tower, I can see the other must-see spots mentioned by the tourism center. I was standing on one of them. Next up was a village kept in such pristine condition that it is like a walk-through, live-in museum. Then a pair of castles and a "natural bridge" of stone in the forest.

Game on.

Of the many villages that comprise Goriška Brda, Šmartno is among the tiniest and is certainly the best-preserved. As I stepped through an archway and into the main square, my first thought was "this is definitely Slovenia and not Italy." It *looked* Italian, with its cobbles and a café with tables outdoors, but it had none of the chaos. I find Italian chaos to be charming: the bustle, the motorinos zipping by, the jovial salutations, the laundry strung across alleyways. But this was just the aesthetic, perfectly clean and calm. The village is lived-in, and there are restaurants, shops, a wine bar…but it feels museum-y, almost too perfect and with a white-washed polish that recalls those all-white villages on Greek islands.

The church of Saint Martin stands at the center of the village. Saint Martin (shortened to Šmartno in Slovene), Martin of Tours, is a local favorite. He lived from around 336 to 397 AD), he was born in Pannonia (nearby modern Hungary), and so is something of a local boy. He served as a Roman legionnaire in Gaul, which is how he ended up, after converting to Christianity, as the third bishop of the now-French city of Tours. He is best-known for the legend of how he encountered a poor beggar shivering against the elements, and he cut off his own cloak in order to gift it to the beggar, to keep him warm. His name day is November 11, which has become a tradition to celebrate in wine-making regions. Slovenia holds *Martinovanje,* a Saint Martin's Day celebration in which the new vintage of wine is poured and enjoyed (and the favorite repast around these parts is a plate of roasted goose with a side of red cabbage and *mlinci,* which are like sheets of pasta. But historically, the saint's name day was a less happy occasion around these parts. That was the day when payments were due: dowries were paid, debts (with interest) were due, and farmers had to pay rent to their landlords. In this rural region, where cash and coins were rare, these payments usually took the form of produce, grain, or wine. In fact, the most frequent payment method was in Rebula wine, which had a good reputation dating back to the Middle Ages and was a popular beverage in the nearby duchies of Carinthia and Carniola (both now parts of Slovenia and southern Austria). For those who could not pay their rent or could not agree with their landlord on next year's rent, Saint Martin's Day was the day they had to vacate the premises or be chased out. But the negative, economic associations with Saint Martin's Day were counterbalanced by the tradition that the men of the villages would gather at a local cellar and tap a barrel containing the new vintage. It was the moment of truth, to evaluate the quality of that year's wine. A celebration emerged from this habit, with prosciutto and salami served in abundance, and a classic dinner comprised of white polenta and cutlets (venison, hare, or, in recent centuries, turkey), while dessert consisted of roasted chestnuts and a local variety of pears cooked in wine (called *pituralka*).

Thus, it's no surprise to find a church dedicated to Saint Martin at the heart of Šmartno. The current church was renovated in 1899, but a church has stood here since the Middle Ages, and the 14th-century bell tower still stretches skyward beside it. The best local artist of the mid-20th century, painter Tone Kralj, decorated the interior with a series of wonderful paintings of the life of Jesus and Saint Martin, with a particularly striking pair of *grisaille* paintings—paintings in a grayscale meant to look like a painting of stone sculptures.

Beyond the church, I make my way to a historical house that has been preserved as a museum. An old, black-and-white film rolls on a television screen with images from Brda's past, before Miro's wine revolution. Pictures flicker by of apple-cheeked women wearing patterned bandanas, and muscled farmers lifting wicker woven baskets piled high with cherries. The charmingly old-fashioned film assures us that "the women of Brda are just as sweet as the cherries." This house is representative of regional dwellings and has surprisingly interesting didactic material—more interesting than you might think, considering the subjects include chimneys and roof tiles. For instance, larger historical farmhouses would be equipped with projecting roofs that extended far out from the wall. This created an additional room, functioning like a covered terrace, which was invaluable to add living and working space in a region with mild winters and hot summers. Mild winters meant that a lot of time could be spent outdoors, and the projecting roof protected folks from the harsh sun. There were three traditional house sizes and layouts. The simplest was a single room in which families lived, cooked, and cleaned, with the fireplace adjacent to the living and sleeping quarters, which was really just a corner of the one-room cottage. One step up from this introduced an extra room, still open to the main living space but a projection off of it, which was used for cooking, to keep the smoke from the fire away from the living quarters. The most elaborate shape featured two projections off the main space—one for cooking, another for cleaning, so the living quarters was reserved for sleeping and daily activities. Wealthier families had a corner of the house called a *šporca* for cleaning: a stone basin to catch water from washed clothes or dishes, and a wooden shelf above it from which a cauldron and a bucket could be hung. If a builder got really creative, they would add a *žbatafur,* which was a projecting corner of the house that functioned as a hearth and chimney combination—it moved the smokiness off to a corner and drew most of the smoke up directly out of the house, whereas the oldest form of fireplace was centrally located, with smoke gradually meandering up to the roof and out of a hole that functioned as a proto-chimney.

As some farmers enjoyed more success than others, houses expanded from this basic, archaic format to include a second floor (usually accessed by an external staircase, with poultry houses underneath). After the First World War, the biggest advance in housing was a shift from open hearths for cooking indoors to brick stoves with chimneys drawing the smoke directly outside. It was not exactly a center of progress, and this historical tidbit indicates just how humble the region was. It was only common for houses to have stoves after the Second World War—at a time when American houses were being equipped with televisions and vacuum cleaners, Brda was just shifting from open fires to stoves for warmth and cooking.

Wineries emerged from this sort of primitive-sounding arrangement of ancient-style houses. The earliest wine-making complex came from the Movia family in the village of Ceglo. Over many decades, one adjacent house after another was built or acquired, until a compound of buildings was unified into a residence for the family and agricultural buildings for winemaking. This tradition of compounds of houses mixed with business dates back to the Roman Empire, when the Barbi family set up a house and ceramics factory (specializing in amphorae, vessels for transporting wine or olive oil) where the village of Neblo now stands. This was part of the Roman state called *Venetia et Histria* (Veneto and Istria today) and was a stop on the trade route from Utinum (Udine today) to Aquileia, an important city for the empire, and one of the largest in the world circa 200 AD, when it boasted a population of 100,000. Brda has been settled since around 2000 BC, as archaeological evidence of Bronze Age settlements has been found, log cabins built on stout wooden piles. It was during the Roman era that the region was more fully settled, with the earliest houses sited on flattened terraces on the southern side of hills—this is still where the best grapes are grown, so the ancients obviously knew what they were doing. They were also growing wine here, even back then. Grape seeds were found inside clay storage vessels in ancient Roman ruins.

From Roman times on forward through the Habsburg era, foreign noble families owned most of the land in Brda. A local version of the feudal system was in place, called the colonate (*kolonat*), in which families rented land (their homes and farming terraces) in exchange for a percentage of what they grew, which would be passed over to the landowner in lieu of cash rent. It was as late as 1947 that this system was abolished, centuries after most of Europe slaked off the feudal system, and decades after the Russian Revolution. Change has always come slowly to this beautiful corner of the globe.

The Second World War was cataclysmic for the region. As mentioned, for more than a thousand years, Brda was seamlessly connected with Italian Collio. Everyone in the area spoke both Slovenian and Italian. There was no delineation in terms of traditions and cultures. Then a pair of wars decimated the local population. The First World War was particularly bloody here, the infamous Isonzo Front (made famous by Ernest Hemingway's novel, *A Farewell to Arms*). But it was the border established after the Second World War that really cut deep and cut off Brda from its neighboring social, societal, and trade partners. Seeing no way out, much of the population of Brda emigrated (heading off to find work in industrial centers), leaving parts essentially uninhabited. Young Yugoslavia had an uphill battle to establish itself as a functioning nation after triumphing in the Second World War, and the cost of their guerilla victory over the Axis was an infrastructure that had not been particularly well-groomed since the region was run by the Austro-Hungarian Empire, and which was torn to shreds by the pair of wars. Sanitary and hygienic facilities were almost non-existent and the region, on the periphery of Yugoslavia and largely overlooked, was plunged back into a sort of Dark Ages. It took decades to see gradual improvement, with the introduction of municipal facilities. It was slow and began from a point of true poverty. It was in this setting that Miro was raised. It was this devastation, hopelessness, and poverty that he saw and was determined to alter for the better.

An imposing, square castle, pinned on each corner by rectangular towers stands just a few minutes away from the Medot winery and Klet Brda. Dobrovo Castle oversaw this area from the start of the 14th century, though the current incarnation dates from the first half of the 17th century and was not a fortress, but rather an elegant residence of Count Colloredo. This family held the territory around Dobrovo since the early 16th century. In 1798, Janez Krstnik Catterini von Ezrberg II bought the castle, and it passed through marriage to the aforementioned Count Silverij de Baguer, when this Spanish, Habsburg ambassador to the Holy See wed Cecilija de Catterini Erzberg. Count de Baguer has a special connection to the Simčič family, specifically to Miro's grandfather, Jožef. The story involves Jožef's role as a soldier for the Habsburgs in Mexico during the ill-fated campaign of Archduke Maximilian von Habsburg to solidify his claim to being not only Archduke of Austria but also Emperor of Mexico.

The brother of Habsburg Emperor Franz Josef was a rear admiral of the Austrian navy and governor-general of the Lombardo-Venetian kingdom, which was part of the Habsburg Empire. But in 1863 he was offered, and accepted, the throne of Mexico, believing (incorrectly, as it turned out) that the Mexican people had voted and chosen him as their leader. In actuality, this was all a trick cooked up by a constituency of Mexicans and French Emperor Napoleon III, who both wished to overthrow the current president of Mexico, Benito Juarez. Napoleon gave the false promise of French military support, and so off Maximilian sailed to Mexico with an army. It was all going well at the start. He was crowned on 10 June 1864 and planned to rule benevolently. He saw himself as a protector of the indigenous groups in Mexico, he maintained the reforms that had been put in place by the liberal president Juarez, whom he deposed. But the treasury was so empty that he had to pay out of his own pocket for the expenses to run the nation. For the time being, Maximilian was assisted by French troops, who drove Juarez northward and kept him out of power. Things might have continued to go well enough, but the American Civil War ended in 1865 and the United States saw the French army's presence near the border between Mexico and Texas as a sign of impending invasion. They demanded that the French remove their army. Carlota, the daughter of Leopold I of Belgium and Maximilian's wife, rushed back to Europe to ask Napoleon III and Pope Pius IX to keep the French army there to support her husband, but to no avail. The French withdrew their army in March 1867 and this allowed Juarez and his army to reclaim their lost territory and recapture Mexico City. Maximilian refused to give up his claim to the throne. He decided to hold his ground with his small imperial army, but they were surrounded and starved out. He surrendered on 15 May

Dobrovo is the center of the Brda wine-growing area.

The Coat of arms of the de Baguer family still visible at Dobrovo Castle

1867 and, despite the pleading letters from many of Europe's leading lights, from Victor Hugo to Giuseppe Garibaldi, Juarez had Maximilian executed by firing squad on 19 June 1867.

Why this historical interlude? Because Jožef Simčič was one of the members of that small imperial army to accompany Maximilian to Mexico…and one of even fewer to survive and return to Europe to tell the story.

Igor Simčič explains: "My great-grandfather, who also lived on the same hill my father did, was forced to travel with Austro-Hungarian Emperor Maximilian to fight in Mexico. He set off with the army from Miramar Castle, near Trieste. The ships left for Mexico. The campaign was an infamous catastrophe. Emperor Maximilian was killed and very few of his soldiers returned home. But as fortune would have it, he was one of the ones who survived and returned. His name was Jožef Simčič. When he came home, he was a big attraction. He'd had these amazing experiences and seen unfathomable sights. In the evenings, people from around our region would gather to ask him questions and hear his stories. At the time, the local noble who has a castle in Brda, Count Bagueri, came to him for advice. He must have seen him as a man with worldly wisdom and experience. He once confided in my great-grandfather that he had fallen in love with a servant girl. He asked what he should do? And my great-grandfather said, 'You must listen to your heart.' And the Count did so and stayed with the servant girl." It's nice to learn that, regardless of one's stature, whether king or peasant, problems are always the same.

Not far from Brda, in a village (population 143) called Hrastovlje, there is a Romanesque church called Holy Trinity. The unprepossessing interior, fortified against Turkish incursions in the 15th century, contains one of the world's great art historical treasures. It is an example of a "Dance of Death" fresco cycle, painted across seven meters of wall and only rediscovered in 1949, when restorers found it hidden beneath a layer of white plaster. The subject, which can be found throughout Europe, is a parade of people from all walks of life, from king to peasant, being led into the afterlife. The theme is that death is the great equalizer, regardless of your social status during life. Well, we might also say that love is the great equalizer, bringing together Count and servant.

At his castle, in 1885, de Baguer set up an elaborate museum collection (consisting of over 600 objects at the time) in the castle, some of which is still on view today in the modest museum found within. Treasures include rare prints, books, and memorabilia, including handwritten notes from the likes of Garibaldi. Most of the collection was shifted to the regional museum in Gorizia prior to the First World War, for fear of damage and looting. Indeed, the castle was taken over as a barracks for Italian soldiers. During the Second World War, in 1943, what treasures were left in the castle were looted, with an estimated 2000 objects taken. The top floor of the castle is now dedicated to a display of 134 prints by Zoran Mušič, Slovenia's most celebrated 20th-century graphic artist, who was born in the village of Bukovica, near Gorizia and Goriška Brda. These were made between 1949 and 1984 and were gifted by the artist to the township of Nova Gorica, which currently operates the castle. The castle has a room that attempts to reconstruct the lost collection and includes an 1885-printed catalogue of the collection's contents.

Now an elegant, luxury, boutique hotel with an impressive restaurant run by chef Mitja Humar (the only one in Brda to be included in the Michelin Guide), the Gredič manor house was first built in the 17th century as a rural retreat. "Gredič" means fortress, but the design of the current structure makes it clear that this was never meant for fighting. Relatively large original windows, angled rather than rounded corners, and only a single tower mean that it would not put up much of a fight if attacked, so the name likely refers to an earlier defensive structure that was later replaced by the current, more sophisticated manor house. The tower, however, may be a holdover of an earlier period—it is needle-thin, consisting only of a spiral staircase, and the staircase winds counterclockwise as you descend. This is a clue for architectural historians. Military structures have spiral staircases that are descended counterclockwise, while residential structure stairs tend to spiral clockwise. The reason is one of logistics in defending such buildings from intruders, the thought being that the defenders would be on the upper stories and the attackers would enter from below and try to mount the stairs. Everyone was historically right-handed prior to the modern era. Even those born left-handed were trained to use their right hands, and lefties were considered suspicious (the English word "sinister" comes from the Latin *sinister,* meaning "left-handed"). Soldiers would wield their weapons with their right hand, so spiral staircases were designed so that a defender on a spiral staircase could strike with their sword in their right hand easily, whereas an attacker fighting up the staircase would be encumbered by the central pillar of the staircase as they sought to slash with their right hand. Thus, the counterclockwise staircase may be a clue that the tower, at least, dates from a time when the structure was meant to be defended. Tenant farmer

Gredič is a 16th century villa that was built as the summer home for an aristocrat. Today it has been restored and features a superb restaurant, a rich wine cellar and hotel rooms

Vila Vipolže is an exquisite Renaissance-style villa from the first half of the 17th century which has been renovated into a new regional cultural conference center

houses, as well as the chapel, were originally built in a ring around the main manor house and may have functioned like a relatively informal circular fortification.

The year 1774 is carved into the Palladian-style chapel adjacent to Gredič, so this may have been the year that the building as we see it today was erected. The owners in the past included the Codelli family, and so the building was referred to as Villa Codelli. The Codellis were a fascinating bunch, none more so than Baron Anton Codelli III (1875-1954). A captain in the Austro-Hungarian Army, he served as director of the Duchy of Carniola and a district captain of the Postojna region (halfway between the Adriatic Coast and Ljubljana). He was a polyglot and adventurer, traveling to China, India, and Japan. He studied law after his military career, but his passion was inventing. He filed patents for early electric vehicles and designed motorboats, rotary engines, lawn mowers, and much more. He was most enthusiastic about the fledgling automobile industry, and he drove the first car in Slovenia, a Benz Velo Comfortable (which was probably not all that comfortable), a proto-car that looks like a stagecoach on bicycle wheels, which he took from Vienna to Ljubljana in 1898.

Gredič was renovated in 2012 and is the best boutique hotel in the region, featuring a spectacular vinotheque tasting room, accessed by a striking concrete ramp, where tastings of wines and sparkling *penina* are held.

Vila Vipolže, the most important building in Brda, was renovated in 2018 and is now home to a fine restaurant, a museum, and event spaces, such as the annual Rebula Masterclass, which is held there every August (of which you've read already). It was built as a hunting lodge for the Counts of Gorizia, when this region was entirely rural. Its first known owner by name was Febo della Torre, who bought it on 14 April 1460. The most famous descendant of the della Torre family was Raymond VI, who was official ambassador of the quirky Emperor Rudolf II Habsburg (who had a castle full of natural and manmade wonders, including a giant octopus in a tank and live penguins) to the Venetian court from 1590-1593, and ambassador to the Holy See in 1597. The palace was expanded in the first half of the 17th century, but in a Renaissance style. It was once surrounded by an elegant, cultivated park, of which only the cypress trees remain—the oldest cypresses in Slovenia. The palace fell on hard times in 1800, when a devastating fire broke out. The fire was so bad that, when the building was next sold, to the Attems family in 1801, the purchasers only used it to store produce (mostly wine)—it was considered

Krčnik Park is the perfect spot to find hidden gems of nature when taking a break from visiting vineyards

uninhabitable. The damage was apparently so great that the original palace was deemed unsalvageable. The next owner, Count Rudolf Erard Anton Baron Teuffenbach, decided to build a new, Renaissance-style palace on the property instead of renovating the original. That is what we see today.

Renovation efforts began in the 1960s and have continued, as this was considered the region's architectural gem and the premier site for official events and conferences. The structure looks particularly beautiful since its 2013 renovation, which included the opening of a restaurant run by Tomaž Kavčič, one of Slovenia's leading chefs, called Kruh in Vino (Bread and Wine). When there are special, high-end events in Goriška Brda, this is where they are held.

A meandering drive into the forest, past several more vineyards and farms, led me to Krčnik Park. Zigzagging steps lead down to a series of pools of turquoise-tinted water that has, over millennia, carved out the limestone rock of the base of the Kožbanjšček stream into a 40-meter-long series of flumes, pools, and "bridges" of stone. While it was February when I visited, had I arrived at a warmer time of year, I'd have had the urge to hop down into the pools and slide along the smooth-bore path the water carved over and through the limestone. (I'm not sure that's allowed, so if you, likewise, have a similar urge... well, you didn't get the idea from me).

And thus ends my exploration of Goriška Brda. Sour cherries, dry wine, otherworldly pršut, castles, rolling hills, some intriguing Counts, and a whole lot of wine to be tasted. Woven through with cycling trails (the Giro d'Italia added Brda along its route for the first time in 2021, and I can see why), there is plenty of tourism in the region even before you get to the wine.

But sour cherries and pršut are light bites. What if I'm getting properly hungry?

10

**PAIRINGS:
FOOD
AND
WINE**

PAIRINGS: FOOD AND WINE

When I was growing up, my parents used to take me on food-focused holidays. They'd read about a great restaurant, or often just a great dish, and off we'd go, booking a trip built around eating a specific thing in a specific place. We once drove four hours, from our home in New Haven to Baltimore just to get a bucket of Thrasher's French fries (yes, in America "bucket" is considered a reasonable unit in which to serve a portion of fries). I'd been to Kansas City to eat barbecue at Arthur Bryant's and taste the fried chicken and cinnamon buns at Stroud's, and I'd been to Michelin three-starred restaurants, like Le Taillevent in Paris, to eat their famous crepes Suzette. To the Charneys, travel means food. So while I love a glass of wine, I'd quite like something edible to wash it down with.

So, what do you come to do here in Goriška Brda?

Eat cherries (when in season, the second half of spring) and taste wine. These culinary experiences logically lead to others along similar lines. You come here to ingest delicious, healthy things.

Recall that my earliest pleasures around these parts involved food. Janez Bratovž, aka JB, considered the godfather of fine dining in Slovenia (and a regular on lists of the top 100 chefs in the world), brought me on that tasting road trip to Plešivo Klinec, a restaurant in the village of Plešivo, run by Uroš and Nejka Klinec, where Uroš makes what may be the world's best pršut. But his is unlike anything else: he makes just 80 legs a year, ages them for 4-5 years away from the wind (most pršut around these parts is preserved in shacks that welcome in the *burja* (bora) saltwater wind off the Adriatic. His pršut has all sorts of layers of flavor: it has an umami, gorgonzola, toasted acorn positive funk to it. And you can only eat it there, on his terrace, with a sprawling view of vineyards tumbling out before you, like a carpet partly shaken to unfurl, but with those hilly clumps still visible beneath it. Uroš is an artist: he won't wrap up any pršut to go, because it oxidizes so quickly and loses its beauty and some of its flavor. He is selective as to who he sells it to. He sells to high-end restaurants, but normally only one per city, to keep it exclusive and to share the love around. A Tokyo restaurant wanted Uroš's pršut, but asked that he remove the hooves, because this detail would be a little too realistic for their customers, who want to see a fine leg of prosciutto carved tableside. Uroš refused: "If they came to me with hooves on, they leave with hooves on," he smiled. He once hosted an informal taste test at his restaurant. He invited the producer he considers the finest at making San Danielle Parma Ham in Italy, and a Spaniard who makes *pata negra jamon*, and asked his diners to rate them, as well as his pršut made from indigenous Slovenian Blackstrap (*Krško polje*) pigs, in a blind taste test. That's an event I would have loved to participate in (Uroš won, in case you were wondering).

JB also took me just across the border, to Cormons, to meet Joško Sirk. Sirk's family runs a complex of guest houses and restaurants, one of which has long carried a Michelin star. But Sirk's passion is vinegar. He's part of a "brotherhood" of Italian chefs who comprise the *Amici Acidi* (Acidic Friends or Friends of Acid), who are dedicated to traditional preparations for wine vinegar, which is aged in oak casks and becomes an ingredient with a complexity comparable to wine itself. There Sirk sat us down in his informal osteria, its walls covered with antlers painted in pastel colors and with gilded tips, as he served course after course topped off with a spray of his famous wine vinegar, which adds an intriguing flavor component to everything from goulash to eggs. Dessert was, you guessed it, wine vinegar sorbet.

So, this region is foodie heaven. People come here to hit the vineyards and taste wine. You already know about the wine (and we'll get back to that, of course). But when drinking said wine, what is recommended to eat along with it?

Darinko Ribolica, chief oenologist of Klet Brda, suggests that "food pairings go beautifully with Rebula, with all the most modern preparations. These days we avoid heavy seasonings and aim for the best ingredients in their natural form. This preparation requires a wine like this. Soft, gentle, clean, drinkable. It doesn't overpower. It allows the food to lead."

Silvan Peršolja, current director of Klet Brda, recalls Miro's words on pairings. "Rebula is like a young woman," Miro liked to say. "Light legs, rosy cheeks. It refreshes you." And he would say, "Soča River trout, light food, and Rebula. It raises the spirit and does not weigh down the body."

Ivan Peršolja, president of the Slovenian Sommelier Association, admires its flexibility when it comes to food. "Rebula is a variety with a lot of facets. If you just look at the various Rebula wines that we have in Brda, you can find sparkling, table wine, highest-quality wine, and even sweet ones, by which we mean wines made from the best-quality dry grapes. It has incredible flexibility and ways of making it into wine. The best-known incarnation is as an approachable, fresh, fruity white, with aromas of herb. There's a levity to it, it's easy to drink, and its freshness inspires the appetite. These wines are rich. Recently, in Portorož, we had a dinner with roast beef and the guests all expected us to serve a red wine with it. But we served Bagueri Rebula. It was an amazing combination. The breadth of Rebula means that we could drink only wines made from this grape throughout a meal, from appetizers to dessert. This could be a great ritual."

Attilio Scienza also highlighted to me its flexibility, which he describes as "a question of the genetics of the grape but also the creativity and ability of the vintner. It can be a Champagne-style sparkling wine, a Prosecco-style aperitif, sweet, it can be a wine for aging. Rebula has a nice flexibility and conforms well to various oenological techniques. The same base can be taken in many directions. It's an original wine. It is unlike Chardonnay, Pinot. It has particular characteristics. It has a complex aroma with a bit of toasted hazelnuts to it. It is naturally reminiscent of Burgundian wines that have aged, not the young ones. This toasted hazelnut scent comes from a very specific chemical that is very rare in wines. If I want to test ten white wines, and if I find that hazelnut scent, I can tell you the chemical composition. Chardonnay has it and Rebula. It's not a floral or fruity wine. The hazelnut, chestnut taste remains a bit sweet, and it's normally a bit bubbly. It can be made more austere and flatter in the hands of the vintner."

This comment about toasted hazelnuts intrigued me, so I asked Denis Rusjan if there is a specific chemical found in Rebula grapes that provides this? "What we find in wine, in terms of aromatic profiles, has a lot of factors," he said. "Terroir, what does it give to the grapes, combined with weather? Grapes then have a profile, and the vintner brings these grapes into the winery and, in the fermentation process, can alter or play with aromas and taste during the wine-making process. What we get in terms of a specific aroma, we know what to expect with Rebula. But we need to know how the wine was made and stored in the winery. Does it involve barriques, or special yeast, and so on. Rebula is fresh, mineral, various citruses, but this is not only what is in the Rebula grape."

Okay. But if we say, "this tastes like butter and limes" (as I've heard experts say of Rebula) is that totally subjective or is it our reaction to specific chemicals found in the wine?

"Thank you for this question, because too often in Slovene we speak of 'wine smelling of limes' we should say 'the wine recalls limes,'" Rusjan told me. "During the fermentation process, the wine will yield to the vintner's wishes. Wine doesn't smell like limes, but it can recall the smell of limes."

Is there a chemical reason that one wine works well with one food, or is that just tradition?

"There is a link," he continued. "In terms of chemistry, we talk about sweetness and sourness, and then aromatics. The same with foods. The overall quality, chemically, surely functions well between wine and food."

Which brings me to the point of this chapter: what do we pair Rebula with when it's lunchtime? I'd been doing a lot of drinking for the benefit of this book (not that I'm complaining), but by now I was getting pretty hungry.

So I spoke to Ana Roš about Rebula. Roš is possibly the world's most famous female chef. Born in Šempeter pri Gorici, where Miro briefly worked before returning to Goriška Brda, she was a champion skier, training with the Yugoslav national team, before studying diplomacy. A self-taught chef, she won Best Female Chef in 2017 and her restaurant, Hiša Franko, in Kobarid, Slovenia was awarded two Michelin stars in 2020. Roš achieved international renown when she was featured on Netflix's *Chef's Table* in 2016, followed by that best chef in the world award the year after—a double-whammy that rocketed her to a place among the stars of the culinary galaxy.

"We recently had a Zoom job interview with a Chilean sommelier," Ana said as soon as I called. "We asked him what he knew about Slovenian wines. The only thing he knew was Rebula."

It is already Slovenia's liquid calling card.

"I just opened a bottle of Rebula," she continued, "because I wanted to be inspired when I talk to you. Matjaž Kramar's Atelier Kramar 2018 Rebula—produced by the brother of Valter," the co-founder of Hiša Franko and its resident wine and cheese master. Matjaž Kramar has a vineyard in Goriška Brda where he specializes in orange wines—Slovenia's highest-profile trend (white wines macerated with extensive skin contact, tinting the wine orange and influencing the flavor). It seems that golden wine will be the next big trend—it already is, it just hasn't been given the expansive, proactive and unified branding that "orange wine" enjoyed. Branding beloved Rebula as "golden wine" would likely have a similar effect. But today, Ana was drinking Kramar's golden nectar.

"It is dry but has a very nice maceration. I believe that we should always drink autochthonous varieties. They are our identity cards. A wine like Rebula brings the name of Slovenia, of Brda, to the world. The philosophy of Hiša Franko is to use everything that can survive in the local environment and present it in the restaurant. Our wine list is no different, very local, very Slovenian. Hiša Franko is a restaurant with more than 90% foreign clientele, coming from all around the world. Australians, Canadians, Americans, Scandinavians. They don't come here to drink French wines. Rebula is always high on the wish list."

While Goriška Brda is beloved of foreigners, I wondered what a Slovene from another region thinks of it. "Goriška Brda, for us, is like a miracle," Ana smiled. "We can be there in 25 minutes, coming from our alpine world and so quickly we're in a place that feels like Tuscany, with a Mediterranean mentality. You can't believe that such a wine producing area can be around the corner from the mountains. Brda is like a surreal bubble of happy people and amazing wine and climate."

I was curious to ask a question that probably wasn't on most interviewers' wish lists. What dish did Ana's children like her to make them? She laughs. "We are all happiest when we have pasta with tomato sauce and curd cheese. We make our own tomato sauce, using 800 liters of the best Istrian tomatoes. And my kids like healthy food but they're sporty, training athletics. So pasta with tomato sauce and olive oil and a goat curd cheese. A perfect meal for an athlete."

Well, I'm no athlete (okay, back in my college days I was a pretty ace squash player, but it's been a few decades since then). Still, I'm getting hungry. To taste the pairings in practice, I asked some of Slovenia's most famous chefs to provide a recipe each that they think would ideally accompany a glass or three of Rebula. I also asked them to recommend which Rebula they'd serve alongside their dish.

I've written about food far more often than I have about wine, including several years as a columnist for Fine Dining Lovers magazine. I also served as a jury member for the Slovenian Restaurant Awards, so I'm familiar with the country's top chefs. You've already met Ana Roš and Janez Bratovž, aka JB. We also briefly mentioned the Sirk family, just across the Italian border.

Mitja Sirk is the son of Joško, he of vinegar fame. Their family has run a Michelin-starred restaurant, *La Subida,* for decades and embody the trans-border nature of the region. They are Slovenian but have lived on the Italian side, in Cormons, since after the Second World War. Mitja is a young winemaker who has been called "a young talented wine-maker to keep an eye on" by Aldo Sohm, who was named America's best sommelier in 2007.

Gredič features not only an elegant hotel and a stunning wine cellar (from the perspective of both its offerings and its architecture), but also a wonderful restaurant. It even received a prestigious Michelin plate. It is run by Mitja Humar, a local from Dobrovo. He lives for food—in his free time, he tends to a fruit orchard and makes olive oil. When cooking at Gredič, he used only herbs and vegetables from Gredič's own garden. His menu focuses on the best ingredients of the region, making Gredič the ideal place to taste both the wines and flavors of Brda.

I called upon two other Slovenian chefs, both of whom recently won Michelin stars and both of whom have restaurants near Goriška Brda. Uroš Fakuč is at the helm of the best restaurant in Nova Gorica, DAM. This fish-specialty restaurant prides itself on gathering the best possible ingredients and boasts a wine selection bursting with Rebula. I first ate there with Igor and Simon Simčič, when Fakuč prepared a multi-course meal to highlight their own Medot wines. So often wines are chosen to go with a meal, but when we're in a particular location to study the wine, it stands to reason that the reverse approach should work well: determine the wine menu first and then choose dishes that will best accompany each glass. Fakuč is known for selecting the best possible local ingredients, particularly fish, and knowing how to feature them in a pristine manner, with minimal intervention and maximized refinement.

Tomaž Kavčič is a Slovenian celebrity, the face of several major brand campaigns and another of the country's first Michelin-starred chefs. He runs the bistro Kruh in Vino (Bread and Wine) in Vila Vipolže, but is best known for Grad Zemono, an elegant manor house that is home to his restaurant. Kavčič is playful and charismatic, with a list of celebrity clientele and signature dishes that include a deconstruction of the favorite Slovenian Sunday lunch staple, beef noodle soup.

It is a real privilege to be able to reach out to such world-renowned chefs who have firmly entrenched Slovenia on the culinary map. It's even better to have their recipes hand-picked for this book, to offer you readers suggestions on what to pair with a glass of Rebula.

But I wouldn't want you to think that Rebula is exclusively of the realm of fine dining. That is how it is best-known, but locals drink Rebula, too. So, in addition to famous chefs, I also asked a non-famous *nonna* from Goriška Brda, Marija Kocina.

Locals say, with great affection, that Marija is a *Briška žena,* a proper, old-school housewife but entirely in the positive sense of the word. She is the matriarch of a farmer family, the one who "holds the four corners of the house together," as a Slovenian saying goes, a hard-working good woman who never complains and puts her family first. Her husband was known as a sort of informal butcher in the area. A centuries-old Slovenian tradition called koline saw villagers gather, usually in December, to slaughter a small number of pigs (sometimes just one) to provide meat for the coming year. Neighbors would assist one another—one family with a single pig, another with perhaps two, a third with no pig at all but there to help out. While the slaughter and processing were something that rural families might do on their own, koline were a point of solidarity and a reason to party. Families who participated would be thanked with gifts of meat, which is how some families with no animals of their own (and possibly no money to buy meat) could receive a store of protein. In order to preserve the meat, much of it was made into sausages, pršut, and salami, all of which made it possible to supplement a largely grain-based diet with protein throughout the year. Marija's husband was a specialist in processing meat for koline and would be invited to each local event. He was known as a master of salami, or šalam in local dialect.

I've participated in several koline. I always choose to arrive after the animal has met its maker—that part is too much for me. But I find fascinating the traditions associated with processing the meat and preparing a wide variety of nose-to-tail goodness, with not a drop wasted. Sausages for cooking, air-drying, smoking, blood sausage, pršut, salami, pork knuckle, cutlets, and loins galore. This ain't for vegetarians, but if you're interested in millennia-old traditions of butchery and culinary heritage, this is the place to be. And Mr. Kocina was the man to be with, to learn from the best.

One of the sons of the Kocina family, Sandi, works at the Medot vineyard tending to the vines in the field. He has inherited his father's mantle as local salami ninja. And he learned from the best. Nonna Marija is a heck of a cook, and she's used to serving up filling, generous portions on limited budgets. Whenever her three sons, daughter, and husband returned from the fields, she'd have something hot for them to eat. And the most storied local dish, the one in the hearts of Brda's residents, is called frtalja. It's a type of frittata, bound by the eggs that can be the only reliable source of protein for a rural farmer. From there you can throw in, well, just about anything that you've got on hand. They are most often loaded with seasonal vegetables. Asparagus is a popular centerpiece, or, if you've got it, sliced sausage or pršut. Nonna Marija's recipe focuses on a broad array of herbs. At this point, it should come as no surprise that it goes nicely with a glass of Rebula…

Rebula is not the reserve of high-end restaurants (although it is entirely at home there), but in these parts, it is simply the best of what is local. It's what families serve each other, their guests, and friends. Here's what Nonna Marija suggests.

Herb Frtalja

Ingredients:
6 whole eggs
½ dcl milk
1 tablespoon of plain flour
Salt
Herbs (what you include is flexible, but Marija uses a combination of chives, parsley, lemon balm, fennel, and feverfew)

Procedure:
Whisk all the ingredients together in a bowl. Warm olive oil in a pan and pour in all of the whisked ingredients. Cook in the pan on medium heat until the egg mixture appears to set and firm at the edges, about 2 minutes, then flip over briefly before removing from the pan and plating.

Serving:
Serve with crusty rustic bread and a glass of, well, Marija says that any Rebula will do. But she is used to serving it with Rebula Journey, since her son tends the vineyards of the Medot winery.

* * * * *

Now that you know what a local *Briška žena* likes to cook for her family, here are some more exotic ideas from four of Slovenia's most famous gourmet chefs.

ANA ROŠ, HIŠA FRANKO

Trout, whey, poppy seeds, beetroot, salad of Fallopia Japonica, sorrel, and wild watercress

Whey sauce

3 l whey
1 l cream

Mix the whey and cream in a pot and reduce in medium low heat, stir once in a while so the bottom doesn't burn, and the mixture doesn't boil. Important to not boil it so the reduction doesn't take a deep brown color. Keep reducing until the sugars star to caramelize. You will notice it once the reduced whey has a light brown color, sweet flavor, and creamy texture.

Mint oil

300 g mint leaves
200 g melissa leaves
500 g grape seed oil

Blend all ingredients in a Thermomix at 70° for 8 minutes. Put the mixture in a metal bowl and do an inverted bain-marie. Once the mixture is cold, strain it through a cheese cloth.

Poppy seeds

50 g puppy seeds
In a nonstick pan, toast the poppy seeds in a medium-low heat.

Pickled beetroot

300 g water
200 g red wine vinegar
20 g salt

50 g sugar
8 pieces tonka beans
300 g red and pink beet roots

Mix all ingredients except the beetroot. Bring to boil, let the mixture to cool down. While the pickled base cools down, slice the beetroot in a mandolin into slices of 0.1 mm. Place the beetroot in a glass jar together with the pickled mixture. Use after 2 days.

Trout
2 x 1 kg trout
Fleur de sel
Olive oil

Fish the trout 12 hours prior to service.

Portion the trout fillets in portions of 120 g. Place the trout in a tray with olive oil and fleur de sel in the button. Cook the trout skin side up under a salamander for a minute.

The trout is still red inside but cooked from outside.
Remove the skin.

Plating
10 plants (we use Quickweed, also called *galinsoga* or shaggy soldier)
10 leaves small nasturtium leaves

Heat the whey, place the trout on it, season it with salt and poppy seeds.
Add a few drops of mint oil, the beetroots, galinsoga, and nasturtium.

Serve with macerated Rebula.

JANEZ BRATOVŽ, JB RESTAURANT

Marinated Shi Drum with Olive Oil and Fleur de Sel, Marinated Cucumbers, Japanese Wineberries, and Lime Snow

Ingredients:
480 g shi drum fillets (from a whole fish 700 g, or use sea bass or gilthead bream)
50 ml olive oil (ideally Lisjak brand from Slovenia)
20 g fleur de sel

For the Stock:
Fish bones
Carrot, celeriac, onion, rosemary

For the Lime Snow:
Juice of 4 limes
30 g sugar

Cucumbers:
1 salad cucumber
50 ml olive oil
50 ml fish stock (made using the shi drum bones)
Salt
1 chili

Extras:
32 Japanese wineberries

Procedure:
Fillet the fish, carefully remove all the bones, and cut the flesh into roughly 1 x 2 cm pieces. Marinate the pieces in olive oil with fleur de sel and keep them in the fridge.

Make a stock using the fish head and bones. First soak the head and bones in cold water for 2 hours, then cook with the vegetables and rosemary on low heat for 1 hour.

To make the marinated cucumber, peel and cut the cucumber into 1 cm cubes. Vacuum seal the cubes with the fish stock, olive oil, and salt, then cook for 4 minutes in water at a low boil and cool. This is best done the day before you plan to serve, to ensure that the cucumbers are well marinated.

To make the lime snow, boil the lime juice and sugar on low heat for 5 minutes, then pour the resulting syrup into a plastic container and freeze. Grate just before serving to make lime snow.

Serving:

Place the marinated fish on a plate. Add cucumber cubes with their marinade, the wineberries, and a little sliced chili. Just before serving, add the lime snow. Serve with fresh Rebula.

MITJA HUMAR, GREDIČ

Ostrich Tartare, Artichoke Cream, Beetroot Gel, Poached Egg Yolk and Crystallized Celery

Ingredients:

For the Ostrich Tartare:
50 g filet of ostrich
5 g chives
10 ml extra virgin olive oil
Salt and pepper to taste

For the Beetroot Gel:
50 ml beet juice
0.5 g agar agar

For the Beet Crisp:
50 g breadcrumbs
10 g beet powder
10 g Maltosec (maltodextrin)
2 teaspoons extra virgin olive oil
2 teaspoons water
Salt and pepper to taste

For the Artichoke Cream:
20 g artichokes in oil
5 g cream
Salt and pepper to taste

For the Poached Egg Yolk:
1 egg yolk
1 teaspoon breadcrumbs
Salt and pepper to taste

For the Crystallized Celery:
20 g celery
Salt, olive oil and pepper to taste.

Procedure:
To make the ostrich tartare, finely mince the ostrich with a knife. Chop the chives. Mix the two together with the olive oil, salt and pepper.
To make the beetroot gel, mix the ingredients, bring them to a boil then let them cool. Mix them once more and put them in a piping bag.
To make the beet crisp, soak the beet powder in the water, then mix the crumbs with It. Then add and mix in the other ingredients. Roll the mixture between to sheets of baking paper. Bake for 20 minutes at 130 degrees Celsius. Cool and serve.
To make the artichoke cream, blend the artichoke, salt and pepper. Add the cream while blending. Blend until you have a smooth creamy consistency.
To make the poached egg yolk, season the yolk with salt and pepper and sprinkle it with breadcrumbs. Fry in oil at 190 degrees Celsius for 30 seconds.
To make the crystallized celery, using a mandolin, cut the celery into thin strips. Place them in a bowl of ice water for an hour and keep it cold until serving. Just before serving, season with salt, pepper and olive oil.

Serving:
Place a metal ring on a plate and press the ostrich tartare into it to form a flat disc. Add four dollops of artichoke cream to the tartare. Place the poached egg yolk in the middle of the tartare. Serve the beetroot gel along the edge of the tartare, shaping it by pulling it with the edge of a spoon. Place two beet crisps into the tartar. Put the celery alongside the tartare. Serve with fresh or mature Rebula.

UROŠ FAKUČ, DAM
Tuna Roasted in a Cuttlefish Crust

Ingredients:
400 g fresh tuna steak
100 g breadcrumbs stained with cuttlefish ink
50 g cuttlefish ink
10 g wasabi
1 egg yolk
50 g flour
1 liter peanut oil
Olive oil
Fleur de sel
Pepper

Procedure:
Cut the tuna fillets into four equal parts. Roll each part in flour, egg yolk and stained crumbs, in that order. Heat the peanut oil in a deep saucepan and fry the tuna in it, stopping while the middle of the tuna is still raw.

Serving:
Cut the tuna into rings, arrange it on the plate. Salt it and drizzle with olive oil. The tuna can be served with a dollop of wasabi and is also good with a side of mashed potatoes flavored with lemon. Serve with mature Rebula.

TOMAŽ KAVČIČ, ZEMONO
"Rice-No-Rice"
Celeriac "Rice" with Trout and a Powder of Tomatoes, Carrots, and Parsley

Ingredients:
1 large trout (800 g to 1000 g)
Salt
Sugar
Butter
Egg white
Potato
Celeriac
Dehydrated tomato
Dehydrated parsley
Dehydrated carrot

Procedure:
Fillet the trout. Set aside the fillets and make a stock out of the leftover parts (the head and tail) by boiling them at a low temperature in water. Cover the trout fillet under a layer of salt and sugar for 24 hours. Then smoke the fillet and cut it into bite-sized pieces. Add some cooked potato, butter, egg white, and puree. Fill the cream whipper with the mixed ingredients and use this to make a "trout foam." Cut a raw celeriac into small pieces (the size of corn kernels). Cook for 25 minutes in the fish stock. The celeriac will visually look like rice and have a similar al dente rice consistency. Dehydrate cubed tomato, carrot, and some parsley, then pulverize in a spice grinder.

Serving:
Put the trout foam on the serving plate, "celeriac rice" in the middle of the foam, and sprinkle with dust of dehydrated tomato, parsley, and carrot to top it off. Serve with macerated Rebula.

MITJA SIRK, LA SUBIDA
Rebula Flour and Pomace
(Recipe provided by chef Alessandro Gavana)

Ingredients:
200 g flour with dried, milled Rebula pomace (the solid remains of grapes after pressing)
2 eggs
4 small zucchinis
1 apricot
A handful of basil leaves
60 g butter
Broth to taste
Salt and pepper
Pinch of garlic powder
Montasio Stravecchio cheese to taste

Procedure:
Make the tagliolini pasta out of the flour mixed with dried, milled pomace from Rebula grapes. Pile the flour on a dry surface, preferably wood. Make a well in the center of it and crack in the eggs. Mix the egg and flour to make the pasta dough. Use a pasta machine to flatten the dough, then cut into long, thin strips. Cook the noodles al dente.
For the sauce, place a knob of butter into a pan, along with a pinch of garlic. When it's bubbling, add the zucchini cut into small slices, but leave out the zucchini's white core. Season with salt and pepper and deglaze the pan with some broth. Add apricot slices and the al dente cooked noodles to the pan. Cook a bit longer in the pan, then top with julienned basil.

Serving:
Place the pasta in a twist at the center of a plate and top with three flakes of Montasio Stravecchio. Serve with macerated Rebula.

11

THE
REBULA
JOURNEY
COMES
FULL
CIRCLE

THE REBULA JOURNEY COMES FULL CIRCLE

I've eaten (though there's still room for more). I've toured. I've interviewed. And man, have I sipped (and occasionally spit). But my Rebula journey has not yet reached its final port of call. I've learned so much about the region, the grape, and Miro Simčič that I must end my grand tour where he ended his: at his private home winery, Medot.

I recalled the label of the Medot Rebula Journey wine, which features a map of the path we were now driving, from Klet Brda winding our way through various local sites linked in some way or another to him and his web of influence. I was literally tracing this journey, moving parallel to Miro.

Medot is perched on a promontory with striking views towards Nova Gorica in the distance beyond a series of vine-clad hills overlapping each other as far as the eye can see. The winery was renovated in 2004 and again in 2019, its grounds strewn with lavender and olive trees (an echo of the south of France, where Igor spends most of the year). We met Simon Simčič, the owner and Igor's son, and Luka Ribolica. Now 27, he spent his lockdown year hyper-focused on the Medot vineyards. Luka looks the part of a former basketball star who trained daily for eight years before deciding that injuries and lifestyle pointed him in another direction, that of the family business. He apprenticed at his father's side as Medot's oenologist and then took the lead role, which he now drives with the professionalism and knowledge of someone twice his age. Luka is truly one of the brightest young lights of the oenology world. I was eager to taste the Medot lineup with their architect, as it were, beside me.

But first, lunch.

Mineštra, a smooth, green minestrone dolloped with cream. Fettucine with pesto. Tomatoes and mozzarella. Goriška Brda is, gastronomically and geographically, a mixture of Italian and Istrian/Slovenian (with a waft of Austrian floating in from the Alps), and this can be seen on its plates.

Writing a book about living people is a special process. Most of my books are about artists long-deceased, or they involve a picaresque of case studies involving criminals I've never met (and probably wouldn't want to, even if I could). What I particularly like about book projects outside of my normal art history and art crime specialization is the chance to dip into research, learn about new fields, and engage with people I might otherwise not have the chance to meet. This book has been one such delight. I now know Goriška Brda better than perhaps many locals.

Medot, where the father of Rebula, Zvonimir Simčič, was born

Three generations: Igor Simčič, Zvonimir Simčič and Simon Simčič

The same goes for Rebula wine, which many will have tasted but few know anything about. For me, the greatest delight has been in spending time with the "family": the people who knew and admired Miro and who continue his legacy. I've been particularly lucky to spend a lot of time, over several years, with Eldina and Simon, and I consider them friends more than clients. Luka can be added to that shortlist. So, the lunch break, prior to an informal tasting, was almost like a family reunion, particularly after a year forced apart by the pandemic.

As we toured the winery, Simon explained that they keep with Miro's preference of shifting grapes from one container to another at a minimum, to preserve the fruit intact until the pressing. "My grandfather used to say," Simon begins, "that once you cut the grape in the vineyard, all you must do is preserve its goodness, its state at the particular moment you cut it. This means that the time from the moment you cut it to the moment you press it should be as short as possible. This is, of course, for sparkling wine, when there is no maceration." At Medot, they start harvesting around 6 AM or a bit later, when the dew has dried, and they press soon after, usually beginning around 8:30 AM. The pressing program (everything is computerized these days) lasts 2.5 hours, so they have the next full load of grapes ready to go around 11 AM. I always thought of the harvest and pressing as a slow, meditative process. Certainly not here. It runs like clockwork.

They use dry ice in the press, at -78 degrees Celsius, to cool down the grapes. Once in the tanks, they remove the oxygen by replacing it with argon gas, thus avoiding oxidation. They soft press immediately, pass the grape must through a series of pipes, which bring down their temperature to avoid any premature fermentation, and the juice enters a series of space-age-looking metal containers. "Then Luka takes it from there," Simon smiles.

Luka also begins guiding our tour. "This is where primary fermentation starts, then the wine is left in the tanks until January," so from the harvest in September or October for several months, before they begin bâtonnage. This process involves stirring settled lees, the sediment derived from the winemaking process (mostly yeast with perhaps some grape seeds and some solid grape particles that didn't get completely crushed), back into the wine. The lees are packed with flavor and are later either filtered out before bottling or left inside if the wine is "racked," or moved from one container to another, leaving the sediment behind, a bit as you might separate an egg yolk from the white, leaving the white behind in the shell. You don't want the lees to remain with the wine indefinitely, but it's up to the oenologist to determine how long they remain in contact and when to remove them.

"Miro did not invent technological breakthroughs," Simon clarifies, "but he brought such breakthroughs with him from his study abroad that the region had not known. So he introduced Yugoslavia to modern wine-making techniques. There was no organization of larger wineries at the time, so he established a system that others followed and learned from. This started with ensuring the quality of the grapes brought into the winery. What to plant, how to plant it, when to plant and harvest. A systematic and strategic approach to the whole operation. He rewarded farmers who brought higher-quality grapes and motivated them to work harder and produce better fruit, which was unusual for the time. During Socialism, in principle everyone had to be equal. So if you gave someone more that didn't sit well. He worked hard to shift this mentality in order to reward those who worked harder and produced better grapes. Treating everyone equally is fine in theory, but it meant that there was no motivation for a farmer to do any more than the minimum required. He also implemented a methodology for producing Rebula wine that led to its international acclaim. The first big award that showed the fruit of his efforts was a gold medal for Rebula at a big international wine festival. He kept winning them from that point on. It grew from there until his retirement, when Rebula was considered among the best white wines available."

So much of this story is about heritage, in the various senses of the word. The heritage of generation after generation inhabiting the same beautiful landscape. The heritage of an ancient, indigenous grape variety at its best where it was always at home. The heritage of long, slow, detailed, centuries-old wine-making techniques. And the heritage of a mantle of honor and responsibility passed down from grandfather to son to grandson.

I took the opportunity to ask Simon for some memories of his *nonno*. As a grandfather, Simon recalls, Miro was "Very professional. His approach to being a grandfather was similar to his status as 'grandfather' of Rebula. He did not show his warmth and love through playing with us, taking care of us. He was The Director his whole adult life and he carried on this manner at home. That's not to say that he was cold, or commanded us, but he carried himself with a pride and authority that, organically, we felt that we should respect. He did not speak often, he was not verbose, but when he spoke, we had a sense that we should all listen and that this was a voice of wisdom. As a child, when we spent time together, he never treated us like children. He always spoke to us as if we were adults, his peers. He spoke in a way we would understand, of course, but he never spoke down to us. But he was always serious, and we really respected him. He was incredibly honest and open. A man of honor. To do something successful, you have to do it without lying, without taking shortcuts, and with a professional etiquette. That absolute professionalism and honesty is something I hope to pass on."

With so many tales of Miro as an exemplary boss, employer, and friend, I'm curious about what memories Simon cherishes of his grandfather as, well, a grandfather. "My fondest memories with my grandfather are when he would take me down among the vines. There was one time in particular, I think I was fourteen or so, and my Nonnica made a picnic basket—iced tea, bread, two cans of tuna, and some pastry—for our mid-morning snack. And we walked through the rows of vines together, with this basket. We sat beneath two chestnut trees that are planted in front of our family house, beside a concrete table that is still there to this day. He would usually tell me a story from his youth, for instance when his parents first planted the two chestnut trees beneath which we sat, when they were saplings just as tall as he was, aged seven. He took a tablecloth out of the picnic basket and draped it carefully over the table. And there we ate together. Those fifteen or twenty minutes together eating was a precious time."

With these images of Miro in mind, now it's off to the Medot archive, where approximately 100 bottles of all of their vintages are aged indefinitely. It is a history of Miro and Medot and Klet Brda in physical form, the best vintages from both cellars (from Klet Brda the stars were Merlot 1966 and 1983 and 1994, Pinot Noir and Cabernet Sauvignon 1994, Tokay 1988, and Rebula 1991) with beautiful bottles housed horizontally in pull-out wooden drawers, with some exhibits tucked in among them, including a vitrine containing objects from Miro's past (a tasting cup, a copy of his book, his insignia as a Knight of Wine in the European Order, a bottle of the first Medot sparkling wine ever made, in 1987, featuring a caricature of Miro himself on the label). "Nonno had two passions regarding wine," Simon says, "Rebula and Champagne." Across from it is another vitrine containing a facsimile of the handwritten instructions, diagrams, and notes of Count de Baguer on the process of winemaking. Explaining every step in a manner so clear that it could be used as a school textbook. I can attest to the fact that the Count had very nice handwriting.

This is also where the wines are tasted before disgorging, to see how the aging evolves. And speaking of tasting...

* * * * *

You may have noticed that I've not really gone into Medot's wines, despite the myriad tastings thus far. I saved them for the end, since they are symbolically the pot of gold at the end of Miro's rainbow Rebula journey. I'd tasted all the Medot wines before, but never in the company of Simon and Luka.

Luka started his professional career at the Medot winery and later moved to Klet Brda, but remains part of the team of oenologists. That team consists of Simon, Luka, Luka's father Darinko (a Rebula specialist), and a well-known oenologist from Champagne in France, Pierre-Yves Bournerias (who is, unsurprisingly, a specialist in sparkling wines). Simon, as befits his title, oversees and weighs in, but leaves the big decision to the three seasoned experts. It is interesting that those experts don't always agree on which direction a certain vintage should be taken. There is plenty of science to winemaking, but the sum total is not the fruit of a mathematical equation. Opinion, taste, and philosophy play important roles. When the three oenologists cannot agree, Simon steps in to make the executive decision of which option to choose. "When the right direction is not quite clear to me," Simon says, "I try to imagine what my grandfather would do. I try to gain as much inspiration as possible from his persona. Medot is very unconventional because it is made like a premium champagne, but primarily with Rebula. So the combination of all three oenologists is what makes Medot special, unique."

We began with Medot Brut 48. This is the only member of their lineup that uses Miro's own recipe. 60-20-20, Rebula, Chardonnay, Pinot Noir. "This is our entry level *penina,*" Luka explains. "The first released by Medot, the one using Miro's recipe. It's aged for four years, made with the classical method." When Miro retired from Klet Brda and established Medot, it was his personal playground. He could now experiment and develop precisely what he wished. That meant no longer using the shortcut Charmat method for introducing bubbles but climbing in the V12 engine race car and using the traditional method that the big boys in Champagne employ.

Sparkling wine based on Rebula, still using the same receipt imagined by Zvonimir Simčič in the 1980s, when he pioneered the classic method of making sparkling Rebula

On a terrace at the top of the Medot vineyard, surrounded by the oldest vines, is the perfect spot to enjoy some serenity, the sounds of the nature and, of course, a glass of Rebula

It's useful to understand the differences. Both begin with a base wine, usually a blend of varieties fermented as you would a still wine. Yeast and sugar are added to a small portion of the base wine and mixed together. This is called liqueur de tirage and it is added back to the base wine. So far, the methods are the same. Next comes the secondary fermentation, during which the yeast converts the sugar in the wine to CO2, carbon dioxide, and alcohol. This can take place directly within the bottle, as it does at Medot, or in a tank. From here on, the methods differ.

The tank approach, the Charmat method, sees the wine undergo its secondary fermentation in a stainless-steel pressure tank. The pressure speeds up the process, much as a pressure cooker would speed up cooking, resulting in a complete secondary fermentation in between one and six weeks. This is far shorter, less fiddly, and less expensive than the traditional method, and so it's good for inexpensive sparkling wines, Proseccos for mixing cocktails, and the like. The result is generally considered less sophisticated, less subtle, less desirable. The traditional method, a la Medot, sees the secondary fermentation take place within bottles, which are aged as little as nine months but often for many years.

The riddling process likewise differs in that the Charmat method requires no riddling at all. The wine is just filtered from the giant steel containers and bottled, with the filtering process removing the lees. The traditional method requires the elaborate and slow riddling process I was introduced to on the Medot tour. At Medot, Simon and Luka, together with Darinko and Pierre-Yves, will taste the non-disgorged wines at least twice a year, to determine when the disgorging should take place and whether they should be placed *sur point,* upside down (riddled), so that the yeasts will concentrate in the neck of the bottle. In addition to helping to get the bottle ready for disgorging, riddling also slows the aging on the yeast.

The next step is called "disgorging" and here, too, it is only in play in the traditional method. Skipping the riddling and disgorging contributes to the speed and low cost of producing sparkling wine with the Charmat method. For traditionalists, disgorging is done on a machine that freezes the neck of the bottle, encasing the lees in ice to easily remove them with this ice lozenge formed in the bottle's neck.

The vintner's stamp is further felt in the "dosage" stage. Here Luka can add a second liquor, made of still wine and sugar, to each bottle. This both replaces the wine lost in the disgorging process and touches up the flavor and aroma, like a chef adding a dash of spice and sauce to finish a plate. Sweeter wines will have more sugar added here, but Medot is all about Brut, extra Brut, and "wow that's dry," which is a mark of sophistication among aficionados. Charmat-method sparkling wines also will receive a dosage, but it is normally added to the wine while it's still in the bulk steel container, not bottle by bottle.

It's clear from these steps how much more labor and time goes into traditional method sparkling wines, hence the higher price and greater prestige.

As I taste the Medot 48, I'm struck with how inexpensive wines like this seem now that I am aware of the expansive effort required to make each one.

One of the keys is just the right level of bubbles. Charmat-method wines are usually fruitier, with larger, rougher bubbles that kick. You can spot a Charmat wine just by bubble-spotting. Traditional-approach bubbles are little sparkles of fun, tight and tiny ticklers. You don't want the bubbles to kick at your nostrils, as they can with seltzer water, for instance. They should be small, tightly wound, and plentiful, bubbling a long time, not only when you first open the bottle. In Italian sparkling water you can order *frizzantissima* (super bubbly), *frizzante* (bubbly), or *legeramente frizzante* (lightly bubbly). I, for one, want my sparkling water to be *frizzantissima* but my sparkling wine should be *legeramente frizzante*. "The foam consistency and long presence of the bubbles are what to look for," Simon says. "You can improve this or make it worse, depending on how you pour it, but what's important is when it disappears." The 48 offered all this, and I could hardly imagine that it was Medot's entry level, when it was so good.

The Extra-Brut Cuvée followed, made of Chardonnay and Rebula (Cuvée means "a tank of wine" in French, but it usually refers to a wine comprised of a mixture of grape varieties). With only 2.5 grams of added sugar in the dosage stage (no sugar is added until that point in the process), I joked that this could be advertised as their "diet" option. I wondered if they'd considered making a Brut Nature, with no added sugar at all. "This is a wine that is ever more popular, because low sugar or no sugar is trendy. But when you make a wine with no sugar, you must be very careful to maintain balance and harmony on your palate when you taste it. Brut Nature wines are usually very vertical, very fresh in the mouth but very short in aftertaste. Fruity, acidic, but without the strength, endurance and subtlety of longer aged sparkling wines. It is very hard to make a wine that is full in your mouth, with a long aftertaste, but with no or low sugar. Only ten, maybe fewer, houses in Champagne have good Brut Nature offerings."

While the previous smelled sweeter, this was pure, clean yeast, as if someone had left dough to rise at the far end of a dark but welcoming cellar. "This is typical, as it has longer fermentation," Simon added. "This was almost five years in contact with the yeast." This was the first of the Medot wines I tasted that were designed by Darinko, Luka, and Pierre-Yves. Only the 48 retained Miro's recipe.

Rosés are supposed to be sweet and airy and simple, right? Not the good ones. This Brut Rosé is a very pale pink, almost "orange wine" color. It's sweet*er* but it isn't sweet. Made of Pinot Noir (60%), Rebula (20%), and Chardonnay (10%), Luka describes it as "the most dramatically different of all other rosés, at least those in Slovenia. Ideal for food pairings." Six-year fermentation leads to a "brioche and cream" taste, as Luka suggests—and I'm happy to agree. Something about describing wines makes me hungry.

"Rosés are normally very pink, fresh, fruity," Simon explains, "but this one has a lot of onion-y notes in the pink. There's more salt to the taste, also thanks to the longer fermentation. A gourmand's rosé." In collaboration with a chef, Simon and Luka organized a menu that would ideally suit a tasting of Medot sparkling wines. Logic would dictate a white fish, perhaps salt-baked sea bass, maybe something as robust as tuna steak or salmon. But that was what the chef suggested for the last in the lineup, Millésime. For the Brut Rosé he surprised everyone and served it with...blood sausage. "For us it was a very strange idea," Simon admits, "but the rosés were clearly the best match."

My eyes flit over to Luka, sitting with quiet, smiling confidence across from me. "What's the feeling you get when you drink a wine that you designed?" I inquire.

"It's fantastic," he says. "You can taste the effort that you put in, from the raising of the vines to the harvest, every step through the bottling. The hours and hours you poured into it. And you can immediately evaluate whether you were successful if you hit your target. And when you do, it's one of the most beautiful feelings."

Reading those reviews can be a nail-biting process. Part of it, I learn, is down to the critic's organization: how many wines are they tasting in one day, and where does yours appear on their to-do list? Critics who mean well can sometimes get tasting fatigue. Miro used to say that, if you taste ten or twelve wines in a sitting, that's about as much as anyone can handle. Your sensibility grows dulled and you grow weary, as do your taste buds. Tasters who try dozens of wines in a sitting are unlikely to give them all equal attention and objectivity, especially those later in the session. There's also the little detail that wine is, you know, alcoholic. Even if you're spitting, you consume minimal amounts of whatever you taste. Multiply minimum amounts by twenty, thirty wines and they accrue to much less than minimal. In short, even tasters who spit can be nicely buzzed by the end of a marathon tasting session, which may be good fun but clouds the judgment. I am aware of this having tasted around a dozen wines today.

The last of the sparkling we tasted was the crème de la crème, Millésime. Like the others, based largely on Rebula (this one is 50%, along with 30% Chardonnay and 20% Pinot Noir), it only has 4 grams of sugar per liter. This bottle is home to the best grapes of each harvest. "But if we only make Millésime if the harvest is particularly good," cautions Luka, so there are years when they go without. Luka, Darinko, and Pierre-Yves taste all the fresh wines in the tanks and decide whether they'll make a Millésime at all. Darinko and Luka are the first to volunteer how much they've learned about sparkling wine from Pierre-Yves, just as he has learned much about Rebula from them. On the question of whether to make Millésime, Pierre-Yves is most attentive, and the Slovenian oenologists allow their French counterpart to take the lead here. Just as Luka and Darinko have sampled Rebula their whole lives, Pierre-Yves has done the same for champagnes.

The grape varieties are stored in different tanks and this can mean that the exact percentage included in Millésime differs from year to year. "We always want to take whatever was best that year and highlight it," Simon adds. They'll create a variety of mixtures stepped at different percentages (60-20-30, 55-25-35, etc.) and sample over and over until they've honed that year's vintage to its sharpest point. The primest of the prime selection of grapes go into Millésime, then the rest are distributed to other wines in their lineup. "This is the best that Medot can produce," Luka says with pride. "It is the best presentation of what our terroir provides."

To go with the Millésime, the silkiest, noblest of the lineup, the chef arranged the tasting to have it accompany not just salt-baked sea bass, but also dessert: a chocolate "truffle" with a real truffle inside it. That so delicate a wine could perfectly pair with a flavor bomb of intense dark chocolate and real truffle was another surprise in that robust menu. This is the sparkling wine with the longest secondary fermentation of any in Slovenia. This was named the best sparkling wine in Slovenia and so remains the exemplar.

Passing the torch from generation to generation, from vision to realization:
Simon Simčič, Zvonimir Simčič and Igor Simčič

Medot plates were developed exclusively for Medot and are only served at the homestead

I have an odd fascination with reading menus, often from restaurants I can only fantasize about eating in. So of course, I wanted to know what was on that tasting menu. On the off chance that you, too, have a menu reading fetish, here we go...

Noodles with shallots, butter, and bottarga (cured fish roe)
Rebula Journey
Sea bass carpaccio and scampi with chopped pancake, seeds, and citrus
Medot Brut 48 + Medot Extra-Brut Cuvée
Chilled foie gras with pear compote and saffron
Medot Brut Rosé + Medot Millésime 2012
Tuna tartare in bread, wasabi, roasted pistachio
Medot Brut 48
Scallops on a bed of mashed cauliflower
Medot Extra-Brut Cuvée + Rebula Journey
Krodegin sausage, kale, and roasted celeriac
Medot Brut Rosé
Pulled pork in its own juices in a baguette, egg yolk, mustard
Medot Millésime 2012
Duck breast with sweet potato
Medot Millésime 2012
Chocolate truffles
Medot Millésime 2012

That's twelve glasses of wine to go with nine courses. Yowza.

So, remember that thing about wine tasting and spitting? That, even when you spit out each mouthful, some of it is consumed? I'm vaguely remembering it now—I think I mentioned it just a few minutes ago, but with enough spittings, you're still consuming some quantity of wine. I checked my watch. Hm. I'm supposed to drive myself about two hours to home in the not-so-distant future. I must be wise and play it safe.

Rebula Journey, as I write the only still wine produced by Medot, is the classic. Rebula done right. Luka explains that he traverses the vineyards prior to harvest each year and sections off the choicest-looking Rebula vines to be harvested some three weeks later than the others, destined for Journey. Medot's vineyards include several clones of Rebula, which Luka checks annually to see how they performed. One part of the vineyard is planted with clones from Miro's father's old vineyard—it was Miro himself who selected which vines would be cloned. These are the vines that go into a bottle of Rebula Journey.

It's comprised of Rebula done in three ways: some is cold macerated, which Luka describes as "highlighting the natural character of Rebula, the minerality and freshness." Another portion is fermented in Inox stainless steel tanks, while still more is aged in oak casks. These three are combined to produce Journey, each bringing their own distinctive elements to the party. The result is a showcase of the grape, with a "sapidity" that shines through. That's a word I hadn't known, but it's best described as a combination of mineral and salty—in a good way.

I might make a parallel with Klet Brda's Bagueri, one of my favorites from back at the Masterclass, alongside my top two of the event, Marjan Simčič's 2016 Opoka Grand Cru (that "centurion," winner of 100 points) and Edi Simčič's Rebula Fojana 2017. In my experience, if there's Simčič behind the bottle, you can't go wrong. Journey's label is particularly poignant: a tiny caricature of Miro, setting off on a serpentine path from the cylindrical main building of Klet Brda, past vineyards, snaking up to the Medot Winery on a hilltop. The story of Miro in a bottle. As Simon says, "This wine is dedicated to my grandfather. He's the guy who brought Rebula to Brda. He's the guy who brought Rebula to Medot. He's the guy who planted Rebula in our vineyards, the ones we use for Journey. He dedicated his life to Rebula and for us, as Medot, it's only right to continue his path." Indeed, on the label is the phrase "Inspired by Miro."

But here comes Simon with an offer to share with me a pair of secret weapons. "And now we taste what will come," says Simon. Project X. It's a forthcoming Rebula, a sequel to Journey, their highly rated first still wine that is meant to tell Miro's story in imbibable liquid form. Project X is part of a concept to create three Rebulas that function as a trilogy to this end. I'm a regular drinker of Rebula Journey, when I can get it (it sells out frequently, but I know a guy who can hook me up). Here was a chance to sample Part Two, as yet unnamed. This I could not pass up. Plus, there was a red, I saw out of the corner of my greedy eye. A what, I asked? Yes, a red.

Medot is so specialized in Rebula that it had never occurred to me that they might make a red. Turns out that it's not for sale, just for home consumption. At Darinko's suggestion, during 2015, a great vintage for reds, Simon decided to buy the best available Merlot, Cabernet Sauvignon, and Cabernet Franc grapes in the region, to play with making a red at the highest level.

So, Secret Unnamed Rebula? Six months before the rest of the world can buy it? Yes, please. Followed by Super Secret Unnamed Red that no one but "family" can taste? Why I think I will!

"The idea of this wine is more fortified than Journey," Simon explains. "But as with all our wines, it's not the muscle but the harmony that we showcase." There stands a golden liquor in a clear bottle with no label other than an enigmatic hand-written code on a plain white sticker: T1. This was the Secret Unnamed Rebula. I thought I could detect a knowing glimmer in Luka's eye before I sipped. Man, it's good. If Rebula Journey is the rhythm section of the Medot rock band, then T1 is the lead vocalist. It sings. "It's not the end product, but it has great potential," Simon noted. I'll second that. But if you'd told me it was the finished version, I'd have believed it.

Hang on, why is there a stain on my trousers?

Somewhere between sipping T1 and awaiting Super Secret Unnamed Red, I looked at my trousers. Hm. It seems that, at some point during the afternoon's taste fest, my spitting cobra act backfired. The small, personal black spittoons were user-friendly enough, or so it seemed, but I'd still somehow managed to cover my trousers—worn for the first time in half a year—with spat very delicious wine. In more than one location.

Darn that ricochet. In my attempt not to drool unpleasantly, I spat too ferociously, and the expulsion bounced back. Guess I should've stayed in my pajama pants. Ah well. Life is a learning experience.

It will likely come as no surprise the Super Secret Unnamed Red was amazing. There was that glimmer in Luka's eye prior to my sip-and-spit that said, "I know this is genius and you'll love it." He was right. Maybe Medot should go into the red market? One step at a time. First, they had to come up with name for T1: Secret Unnamed Rebula (it sounds like the title of an action movie). To help absorb the unspit red and hone our thoughts, Simon brings out a šalam. He had just helped to make it this winter, along with Sandi, the salami ninja but also a vineyard expert who cares for and oversees the vineyards at Medot. Together with some Medot staff, who are like extended family, they bury their hands in very cold chopped pork that was living pork but a few hours earlier. They cube the fat by hand and Simon was concerned that the cubes were not of equal size. Well, let's be honest—it was Simon's job to cube the fat, and Sandi was less than impressed at Simon's first attempts. He was also worried that it wasn't dry enough—it could use a few more weeks at least to air-dry. I'm not the sort of guy to worry about such details. It tasted great, and felt great to receive, too. Because one of the local traditions in Goriška Brda is that, while every guest will be offered wine, the guests who are like family are the ones offered the house-made šalam. Šalam was always a rare treat in Brda. Many households made it, but they usually did so in very small numbers. Out of one pig, you might get only around 25 salamis. Considering that they would need to last a family a whole year, each šalam is treated with respect and savored.

After this I quickly shifted from wine spitting to coffee swallowing to get myself back in shape for the drive home. There was but one more question to answer. They couldn't decide what to name T1: Secret Unnamed Rebula. They were toying with Grand Epoch, as the concept was to harken back to the late 70s, Miro's golden age of golden Rebula, but to imagine the wine he would make if he had the technological capabilities available today to oenologists like Luka and Darinko.

"Since the book will be called *Golden Wine,* maybe it would be apt to have the word 'golden' in the name?" I suggested. It doesn't feature in any of the Medot wines, aside from their color when poured, of course. "Super Secret Unnamed Red could be Black Gold," I thought. "But what if, instead of Grand Epoch, you go with Golden Epoch?"

It has a nice ring to it. And this is a perfect place to end our own Rebula journey. The only thing left, now that you know the story of Miro Simčič, Goriška Brda, wine in Yugoslavia and Slovenia, and the treasures of the golden wine, is to visit and taste for yourself. But until you can come to this idyllic place, this cluster of perfect villages perched between the Alps and the Adriatic, cradled by both Italy and Slovenia, you can still drink a glass of Rebula. May it transport you on your Rebula journey.

For me, this Rebula journey has been the most special and in-depth of my many forays into getting to know my adopted homeland of Slovenia. Most of the time I'll explore a new food, festival, or phenomenon for a day or so, do some light research, and write a magazine article about it. That's that. This has been a totally different, far deeper experience. I feel that I've gotten to know Brda to a level of depth that few in the world do—not just foreigners but even Slovenes reading this book will hopefully learn much. Heck, there may even be those of you living in Goriška Brda who will finish this book with a greater knowledge of, and deeper appreciation for, your own backyard. That's my goal as an informal prophet of the wonders of Slovenia, "the world's best country," as I've often called it and have long firmly believed. What a treat to unfold a new geography within this best of all countries, one relatively distant from my home in the Slovenian Alps, and feel that it is a second home, to have developed friendships here with locals, to "read" its rolling vine-clad hills and now to understand the magic of its "poor" soil that yields so rich and celebrated a fruit.

I also feel a closeness to great man I never had the chance to meet: Miro Simčič. History is made not of the acts of kings and presidents, but of thousands of smaller acts with big consequences. Brda is grateful, as the community should be, that a good local boy decided to give back to his once-impoverished home and, for many years almost single-handedly, elevate it through the wealth of fruit from its "poor" soil to a world-renowned terroir and place of elegance, refinement, and beauty. For me this Rebula journey has been a personal masterclass, and it's been my pleasure to share it with you.

And if you, too, come to Goriška Brda, a glass of wine—and a slice of *šalam*—await.

ACKNOWLEDGMENTS

A book is a mosaic of stories, tips, favors, and experiences. The author simply puts it all together. I want to first thank the Simčič family for being driving force behind this project: Igor and Simon, who were so helpful in helping me to tell the story of their *nonno*, Miro. Eldina Domazet was the project's engine—we spent many happy hours driving to and from Goriška Brda, and she facilitated just about every aspect of the research, interviews, and writing.

I'm grateful to all the vintners who offered their time, thoughts, and wine, those affiliated with Rebula Masterclass and beyond. The teams at Klet Brda and Medot took a great deal of time hosting and informing me on the legacy of their founder, Miro. Particular thanks go to those who sat with me for interviews, from winemakers to politicians to experts, from Italy and Slovenia. It was a trilingual project, bouncing from Italian to Slovene to English. Thanks to Josh Rocchio for proofing words in all three. And Caroline Gilby kindly penned the Foreword, as well as offered some editing suggestions that were most valuable.

The beauty of this book is down to the wondrous designs of Žare Kerin (the second of my books that he designed—lucky me!) and the photographers who contributed such wonderful pictures to bring the story to life. Thanks also to the team that runs Rebula Masterclass and Goriška Brda tourism, including the charming mayor, and the world-famous chefs who contributed recipes.

Thanks go to my wife, Urška Charney, who made the elegant map of the region for this book and also helped with countless translations from Slovene into English.

A personal note of thanks to my wife and daughters, who supported Dad zipping off on many occasions to drink wine, with the happy excuse that Dad was writing a book about it. Thanks also to my editor at Rowman & Littlefield, Charles Harmon, who has already shepherded three of my books to successful publication, and we're on track for many more.

Finally, thanks to you, dear reader, for putting up with me relating all these lovely travel, eating and drinking stories! I hope that you had a glass of wine in hand. And for your next wine-themed holiday, consider coming to visit the sunny side of the Alps. You'll find a glass of Rebula (or fifteen) ready and waiting. Only one more phrase to teach you. Cheers: Na zdravje!

Zvonimir Simčič, Medot

SLOVENIA

Krasno

Višnjevik ⑤

Hruševlje

④

Neblo ● ③

① Dobrovo

Šmartno Kojsko ⑥

②

Hum

Podsabotin

⑬

Medana

Plešivo

⑫

⑯ ⑰

⑪ ⑨

ITALY

⑩ Ceglo

⑭

⑦

Vipolže

⑧

⑮

1	Klet Brda	10	Dolfo
2	Medot	11	Marjan Simčič
3	Silveri	12	Ščurek
4	Zanut	13	Jermann
5	Erzetič	14	Kristian Keber
6	Ferdinand	15	Gradis'ciutta
7	Edi Simčič	16	Radikon
8	Moro	17	Gravner
9	Movia	★	House of Rebula

Brda/Collio Ljubljana